GLOBAL VALUES

A NEW PARADIGM FOR A NEW WORLD

KARIN MILLER

Global Values: A New Paradigm For A New World
Copyright © 2015 Karin Miller

All rights reserved. No part of this book may be used or reproduced in any manner whatsoever without written permission except in the case of brief quotations attributed to the author.

www.ournewevolution.org

ISBN: 978-0-9909204-0-3

First Edition

10 9 8 7 6 5 4 3 2 1

CONTENTS

INTRODUCTION 1

1. UNITY 13
2. COMMUNITY 29
3. LIFE 38
4. FREEDOM 44
5. CONNECTION 53
6. SUSTAINABILITY 68
7. CREATIVITY 76
8. EMPOWERMENT 83
9. CHOICE 94
10. INTEGRITY 108
11. A CALL TO ACTION 119

ABOUT THE AUTHOR 133

INTRODUCTION

War, terrorism, economic instability, poverty, crime, unemployment, and environmental crises fill the news. Yet many of us carry on with our daily lives as if everything was fine. We continue to buy and consume more and more. We continue to rely on fossil fuels and unsustainable technologies that pollute our environment and endanger its many species of plants and animals. We continue to ignore the suffering of others in our communities, countries, and across the globe. We have forgotten that we all live on one planet, and that we are all connected. We have forgotten that a crisis on the other side of the world is our crisis one day. It is as if we have all fallen asleep and are dreaming a collective nightmare.

Despite all the troubles we face, there is beauty in this global predicament. The world is at a turning point. These crises can teach us. Rather than causing us to despair or to feel ambivalent, they can bring us hope. They are our chance to make a better world and a better future.

Our current mode of operation—acting in isolation, separation, and only for individual benefit—is not sustainable. While some people may continue to benefit from ignoring the whole in the short run, society will eventually begin to crumble under this paradigm just as a body dies when ravaged by cancer. A healthier approach is to recognize that we are all one body of life. By stretching beyond our personal comfort and satisfaction, we can transition into ways of being that are sustainable, inclusive, and conducive to all life.

The values set forth in this book are offered as the foundation for a new paradigm to help humanity evolve as a species by moving us away from isolationism, separation, individualism, and the destruction that lies ahead on our current path. Changing the ways we interact and live—with each other and all life on the planet—will enable us to find new solutions and opportunities for individual and societal transformation. It is possible to create, and shift into, a new approach that welcomes, values, and supports all perspectives and the beautiful diversity of the world. It is time to wake up and create a new paradigm that supports and benefits the whole body of life. When we embrace the values of unity, community, life, freedom, connection, sustainability, creativity, empowerment, choice, and integrity—what are referred to in this book as "Global Values"—we can create a healthy and sustainable world with real social justice underpinned by democracy and human rights.

How did we get here?

Generally speaking, Western culture moved from understanding the world through myths (mythos) to understanding the world through religion and theology (theos). About 2,500 years ago, with the birth of Western philosophy, the ancient Greeks shifted our thinking toward inquiries about the natural world and the role of humans in it. They nudged Western thinking toward order, reason, and words (logos). Religion continued to dominate Western cultures, but the tendency toward reason was building steam.

By the 18th century, Western society was moving into the age of modernity, and the Industrial Revolution was getting under way. These things changed not only Western culture, but the entire world. The Industrial Revolution brought mass production of consumer goods and mass reproduction of cultural goods, and the age of modernity gave humans a false sense of dominance and superiority over the natural world. Many people came to believe that they could control and conquer nature, and that all their problems would one day be solved by reason, science, and progress.

Today, we are in the Information Age—some call it the Computer Age or the Digital Age. We have certainly made great technological advances, including those that connect us through the Internet, the Word Wide Web, e-mail, and social media. Unfortunately, today's postmodern world is not as successful as many had once hoped it would be.

In our excitement for progress, things seem to have spiraled out of control and our dreams of a better world are like memories from the distant past. Extreme weather and droughts are wreaking havoc across the planet. Clean water is becoming scarce. Advances in medicine are being clawed back by antibiotic-resistant bacteria. We are seeing all sorts of societal collapses, and our communities are being ripped apart at the seams by many social ills. Sophisticated societies have literally been destroyed by war, while others are suffering from failing transportation, education, and health infrastructures. For many communities, long time social inequality is causing civil unrest. As individuals, many of us feel we are living pointless lives focused only on ourselves—and we feel powerless in the bigger scheme of things.

We are living in a time of great turmoil. Many things are changing beyond recognition, or disappearing altogether. Our old social structures are falling apart, and many people are grasping at the pieces to hold them together. In desperate attempts to maintain some stability, people are clinging fearfully to that which is familiar.

Desperation can cause people to become more conservative, more liberal, or more extreme in their values, opinions, and religious beliefs. Some people are even willing to kill and die to maintain their traditions and what they know best. They hope their fanaticism will somehow keep the old ways alive and preserve the world that is being torn from all of us. The problem with extremes is that not only do they not help us, they hurt us. Extreme viewpoints polarize us, causing the gaps between people to grow wider and making it more challenging to find common ground. This does nothing to help us solve our global problems.

We will never get anywhere new by following the liberal left, the conservative right, or any sort of fundamentalism. We have already taken these paths, and each of them has led us to where we are now.

We must "re-member" that we are one.

We have lost our connections with each other and the natural world, and it is time for humanity to "re-member" that all life is one. Our societies no longer value cooperation, kindness, generosity, and compassion. We collectively live in a state of great imbalance, and as individuals many of us are isolated from each other and our communities. If we want to change things for the better, we have to start by changing our own thinking. By changing our minds, and re-membering our connectedness, we can shift our paradigm and support actions that promote a healthy and sustainable world.

Remembering that all life is one is about putting humanity back together again conceptually, and making us whole. It is about realizing we are all interconnected and integral parts of the whole body of life, and reimagining how we think of ourselves in relation to others. It can be helpful to think about humanity as a single human body. If we think about each person as a cell in the body of humanity, it is easy to see we all need to work together. Each cell performs its individual function, but that function is best carried out in cooperation and coordination with other cells for the benefit of the whole body.

Sadly, as things are now, it seems as though we are living in a collective hallucination of disconnectedness. We have lost sight of our intimate and intricate connections to everything and everyone, and we view ourselves as unconnected, lone individuals. It is as if all the cells in the body of humanity have forgotten they are part of a whole—and the cells have forgotten that if the body dies, they too will die.

The pressures of living in this isolated way are pushing our societies and our bodies to their physical limits. Rather than working together for the benefit of all, our societies are in fierce, often deadly, competition for vital resources—energy, water, food, shelter. As individuals, we are in competition with each other for jobs and income so that we can secure vital resources for ourselves and our families. If we are lucky enough to have a job, we are working longer hours, spending more time away from our loved ones, and travelling many miles each week just to keep roofs over our heads and food on our tables. This increased individual activity has a negative impact on the environment and our societies. As a result, our habitats, infrastructures, and social systems are reaching breaking point. We live in vicious circles of competition, consumption, and destruction.

The promise of modernity has been broken—things are not getting better. If we are to reclaim our lives, our societies, and our happiness, we have no choice but to change our ways. By recognizing we are all one, we can begin to live in balance with each other and all creation. This is not to suggest that we negate our individuality, give away our money, or act altruistically against our self-interests. Rather, this is a call to act with an awareness of the whole and to remember that we as individuals are part of that larger body of life. We recognize that it is in our own self-interest to align with the interests of the greater whole because we are ultimately connected. What we do for others and our environment directly or indirectly impacts ourselves.

Our journey is like the story of *The Wizard of Oz*.

Like Dorothy Gale in *The Wizard of Oz*, we are all on remarkable personal journeys. Collectively, as societies, we also sought something more fulfilling over the rainbow. However, rather than finding the Emerald City, we have been swept up in a cyclone of chaos—just like Dorothy. Having been knocked unconscious, we now seem to be lost together in a dream. As Dorothy looked to the Wizard of Oz to help her find a way home, we hope for something or someone who can deliver on the promises of a better future, or who can at least take us back to what we remember as the idyllic days of the past. Unfortunately, the wizard was powerless to send Dorothy home, and she had to find her own way, aided by the new friends she makes throughout her journey. Similarly, no magic solutions to our global predicaments exist outside ourselves. We must learn that we have the answers and the ability to get ourselves home. Rather than looking to institutional knowledge and conventional norms, it is time to trust ourselves. We can let go of our old ways and assume a perspective that will lend itself to a sustainable existence on this planet. This is the way to peace and stability for humanity.

It takes both introspection and great courage to change. When we are reluctant to change it is usually because we are holding on to fear. Perhaps we fear losing what we hold near and dear, or have become comfortable with the status quo and fear we do not know what our future will hold for us if things change. Not wanting to make a poor decision, we cling tightly to that which we know best—even if it is not good for us or society. Our resistance to change can paralyze us if we let it. If we want a better world and a better way, if we want to make the transition to peace and stability, we must face our fears. We must admit that things are not working, and that our current approach is incomplete, inadequate, and ill-equipped to deal with all the challenges we are facing in our chaotic world. Like the Lion, the Scarecrow, and the Tin Man in *The Wizard of Oz*, we must find the courage, the intelligence, and the heart to change our ways.

We merely need to look inside ourselves, as Dorothy did, to realize that we have had the answers all along. For example, we know deep down that connection, sustainability, and freedom are more useful to ourselves and humanity than isolation, wastefulness, and bondage. We can choose to discard unhealthy values and systems and embrace—or reclaim—values that support a healthy and sustainable world and that promote peace and stability.

A holistic approach

Hungarian philosopher of science and systems theorist Ervin László suggests that society is at a critical turning point in human evolution. He has suggested we need a social shift toward a "planetary ethics" and responsibility, so we can move into an era of better environmental stewardship, sustainability, and peace. Laszlo describes a form of ethics whereby we should feel responsibility to all, to the whole circle in which we are involved. He says, "Human consciousness can evolve. At the innovative margins of society it is already evolving. A holistic view is taking shape, one that sees the human being as an organic whole, embedded in the socio- and culture-sphere, embedded in turn in the wholeness of the biosphere."

Now is the time to learn from our past and evolve. We can use this challenging point in history to create a new paradigm. As asserted by Alastair Taylor in the early 1960's through a systems-theory model of human evolution, we are uniquely positioned to synthesize what we have learned from the mythos, theos, and logos eras to create a new era based on holos, or wholeness. If we step out of the game, and objectively observe the needs and interactions of all of the players, we can create new solutions for the benefit of all—we can create a holistic paradigm. Such a holistic paradigm will take the whole of life and creation into consideration, and it will recognize the interdependence of all thoughts, actions, and forms of life. It will function as a support for the whole body of life in all its diversity and beauty.

A great renaissance grounded in connection and the need for one another is at hand. It is time to embrace each other and all creation, and to work together in the spirit of cooperation and community to shift into a holistic paradigm that will benefit us all. It is time for us to evolve.

A new paradigm for a new world

This book is intended to promote a shift in human consciousness to a holistic paradigm rooted in Global Values. Global Values serve as a common thread uniting people of all different religions, cultures, and political viewpoints. Rather than asserting truth, they offer a new perspective and platform upon which to base our thoughts and actions. They can inform a holistic paradigm, and they can be embraced by all peoples in order to work for positive societal transformations. Global Values represent a new approach for a new era.

Our current paradigm encourages categorization, separation, and isolation, and it is no wonder the world is in chaos. These values divide people, and they can cause us to turn against each other. The changes taking place in the world in the name of these values are destroying us and our environment. We are living through the dismantling of our old ways, but there is great power in times of change. Chaos is itself a catalyst for change, and it always contains great potential. We can try to turn away or hide from the chaos, or we can awaken our senses and our spirit and face it. When we face chaos with a new aliveness we can see expanded views of the universe, and this makes room for new possibilities—we see we can evolve out of chaos.

The evolution of humanity can be thought of like the metamorphosis of a caterpillar into a butterfly. Once the caterpillar's body is isolated in its cocoon, enzymes are released to dissolve it. The result is a gelatinous goo, a pool of pure potentiality. Imaginal discs are clumps of cells that are not broken down by the enzymes, and they use the caterpillar goo to grow. The imaginal discs grow into wings, legs, antennae, and every other part of a butterfly, and finally, all these parts connect with each other to create the butterfly that will break out of its protective chrysalis and fly off to a new life. Humanity is in the breakdown and transformation stage of metamorphosis. Our familiar structures are falling away, and everything is in chaos. Peace, stability, and order seem to be things of the past. The body of life is being consumed, wars are raging, economies are cannibalizing each other, everything is breaking down, and yet, we are surrounded by pure potentiality.

If we think of ourselves as imaginal discs in mid-metamorphosis, we can think of Global Values as the bit of DNA that will enable us to bind together in new ways, so that we may evolve and emerge from the chaos as a more beautiful incarnation of humanity. Like the imaginal discs that connect in a transforming caterpillar, new technologies have brought us a new awareness of each other and our opportunity as a species. Through our smartphones and other Internet connected devices, we can easily connect and communicate with people from all over the world. We can access and share information as never before. Through social media we may become friends with others whom we have never even met in person. We can share our views on the hot topics of the day at a click of a button. Such new technologies can be used to solve our problems as we join in group discussions of both our communities at home and virtual communities around the world. By joining forces, we can build a critical mass of support for our new evolution to a state of balance and unity.

We now have the opportunity to join together both at the local and global level and collectively act as one for the benefit of all creation. If you are seeking to work together for a sustainable, unified world that reflects the oneness and interconnectedness of all things, please join me and all who share Global Values. Together, we can shift to a new, holistic paradigm that supports a healthy and sustainable world.

1 UNITY

Together we make up one body of life.
Our diversity is a celebration of all that is. Together, we are whole.

Imagine all living things as one human body. The body started out whole, complete, and healthy, but over time it has broken down. The parts have become isolated from each other, and the whole has become fragmented. The immune system is now weakened, and the body has many diseases. War, terrorism, tyranny, climate change, pollution, poverty, and all the other maladies we are experiencing are diseases of the body of life. These diseases are putting our ecosystems—and the entire planet—under great stress. They have truly become a matter of life and death. Now, more than ever, we need to overcome the dysfunction we have created by remembering the unity, oneness, and connectedness of all things.

Our current paradigm supports and encourages separation and isolation, and it is causing great individual and global pain. The body of life is suffering, and the pain we are all feeling is its way of telling us to choose again. It is as if it is shouting at us, "Don't do that!" as we jump out of the frying pan and into the fire. Fortunately, darkness and pain can help us learn and grow. The eventual solutions to the problems caused by our old, misguided actions will likely cause us to change our ways. In other words, when we join together in unity and act as one for the benefit of all life, we will evolve and cure the diseases of the body of life.

The way we live today is harmful for us as individuals, for other living beings, and of course for the natural world. The tapestry of life has been shredded, and it is now a tangled mess of threads. Rather than weaving our tapestry into an intricate masterpiece that reflects the beauty of all life, we have pulled it apart. The future of the tapestry depends on our intentions. We can carry on living with our tangled mess and risk the demise of humanity. Or, in unity, we can weave the tapestry of life back together again—we can create sustainable ways of being that respect and reflect the diversity of all creation, and support the whole.

Some people reject the value of unity—and unity consciousness—because they think it means losing their individuality. This is not the case. Unity is not uniformity. It does not seek to make everyone conform to one mold or one way of being, and it does not mean forcing anyone to accept a single viewpoint. Unity is a coming together of individuals to repair the tapestry of life. It is a weaving together of the many diverse aspects of creation into a cohesive whole. Together, we can support each other in a beautifully balanced society, like a cloth woven of many types of individual threads that is much stronger than any individual strand on its own.

Embracing unity will allow us to overcome our isolation and separation—as individuals and societies. When we value unity, we respect, and live in balance with, other forms of life and our environment. His Holiness the 14th Dalai Lama of Tibet tells us that, "Today, more than ever before, life must be characterized by a sense of universal responsibility, not only nation to nation and human to human, but also human to other forms of life." This message is vital because we are one interconnected body of life, and our actions affect all other living things.

What sort of future will we choose to create? Will we act in fear—from our constricted, isolated, and narrow viewpoints? Or will we join with the many diverse cultures, communities, and viewpoints that surround us? By embracing unity, and unity consciousness, humanity can weave together all the dark and light threads, the coarse fibers and the smooth silks, the bulky yarns and the finest filaments to create a tapestry of life that embodies the great contrast and sublime beauty of all creation.

Many people believe that peace is the solution to the world's problems, but peace is not a means, it is the end result of valuing and living in unity. Peace comes from a realization of the oneness and interconnection of all creation—a realization that the separation and isolation we experience are illusions—and understanding that each person's thoughts and actions have an effect on all things. Peace is the product of unity consciousness and the love that arises from it. It cannot arise out of fear. When we act in fear we produce violence and separation, and we pull at the threads of the tapestry of life.

With unity consciousness, we can become a source of healing—repairing the rifts in the tapestry of life. In valuing unity we step into the shoes of others, see the world from their perspectives, and we respect their needs. The love we generate when we operate as one can change the world. Together, we can become whole and complete once again, and live in peace.

The Industrial Revolution and cultural individualism

The Industrial Revolution began in the late 18th century with the advent of new manufacturing processes and continued through the mid-20th century when society began to shift from industrialization to an economy based on digitized information. During that period of industrialization, society saw great innovations in the areas of textiles, transportation, and iron making (to name a few), resulting in great wealth and abundance in society. The Industrial Revolution spurred major advances in every aspect of life imaginable—technology, manufacturing, agriculture, transportation, communications, engineering, banking, medicine, education, and art.

These changes had a profound effect on Western culture, and on cultures across the world. People migrated from rural to urban environments, often alone and separated from their families. The small home office was replaced by the office building. Many workers moved from farms, small workshops, and cottage industries into large factories. However, surrounded as they were by many other workers, they were often isolated, anonymous cogs in the machines of industry. As technology increased, so did cultural individualism and the belief that we can all make it on our own if we can just work a bit harder and stay in the game.

There is no doubt that these changes allowed societies to achieve great material success, and individuals to benefit from new conveniences, abundance, and wealth. However, with these gains, society in certain respects may have lost sight of the bigger picture. Many of us have become disconnected: both from the majesty and beauty of nature, and also from the people who share our environment. Today, people work in massive business and industrial parks and huge steel and concrete towers—often isolated in cubicles. Through technological innovation we have become masters of categorizing, labeling, differentiating, and compartmentalizing things in order to combine them in new and interesting ways. While this most certainly has its benefits, these tendencies have also led to a predominant worldview based on isolation, separation, and cultural individualism. From this myopic viewpoint, it is very hard even to imagine the unity and oneness of all things.

We have scaled the heights. Now what?

Imagine that you trained your whole life to climb a mountain. You learned about mountaineering, you built-up your strength and practical skills, and you got very good at adapting to the changeable weather on the mountain. Through hard work and perseverance, you finally attained your goal. You climbed the mountain, reached the summit, and now you are standing at the peak. Surprisingly, as you look out at the panoramic view, you find that you are terribly afraid of this new height. You want to bend or sit down to maintain your stability. You were not scared during the ascent. So why are you afraid now that you have reached your goal? You realize that you were so focused on getting to the top—and ensuring the safety of each foothold and step— you did not have time to think, or look around or down, as you pushed upward. Now at the peak of the mountain, your stomach sinks. You are terrified of the height, and all you can do is look down at the ground as the wind swirls around you.

This scenario may sound unrealistic, but many of us are living in this way. We work as hard as we can to achieve success in life. We climb mountains and aim for the top. Our ability to focus on the task at hand has brought us to new heights previously thought impossible. We have reached the peak of material success, and some of us have abundance and personal comfort beyond our wildest dreams.

Our focus and determination may have served us well to achieve our personal goals. Yet, many of us with such abundance find ourselves feeling alone and isolated on our mountain tops of achievement. We have traveled so high— with such a narrow view—we have lost sight of the broader landscape. Valuing individualism has made us strong, and driven us to climb mountains, but if we forget our larger context in the body of life, we can find ourselves separated from and perhaps at odds with the whole of humanity, our environment, and all living things.

Many of us are now ready for a new approach, one that will push us to grow beyond ourselves and our past peaks of success. We may feel paralyzed with fear looking down from this height, but moving forward can be as simple as shifting our perspective. If we muster the courage to look up from the ground, we see the vast beauty of the panorama of life that surrounds us. From this new point of view, we see people who have reached the peaks of other mountains, and those who are traveling at all elevations. We see the plants and birds and animals all playing their vital roles in the balance of the ecosystem. When we look up at the night sky we see endless stars, and we imagine what lies beyond us in the greatness of the universe.

Our world changes in an instant when we recognize the vast diversity of life around us. When we take in the beauty of all life, our mental paradigm of separation and isolation begins to shift. We recognize that we are not solitary players in the game of life. We are on a giant team, and each of us, and all life, has a role to play. If we want to give our team the best possible chance of success, then we must be team players, and we must value, include, and depend on all our team members.

From this new point of view, we realize that the values that pushed us as individuals are important, but they are only pieces of a greater puzzle. With a broader perspective, we see that we all inhabit many interconnected systems—ecosystems, societies, religions, cultures, workplaces, sports teams, families—that are all part of an enormous system. In heightened consciousness, we begin to understand and value the unity and interconnectedness of the universe. We recognize that—together with all of creation—we are whole.

Is it really just a matter of changing our perspective? Yes. Is it easy? No. The shift from an individual perspective to a unity perspective is like moving from a belief that the Earth is the center of the universe to a knowledge that the Earth revolves around the Sun, our star, and that our solar system is in a minor spiral arm—the Orion Spur—of the Milky Way galaxy that contains an estimated 200-400 billion stars, many of which have their own planets. As we expand our perspective, we realize that not only does our galaxy contain billions of stars and planets, but it is estimated that there are billions of galaxies with hundreds of billions of stars in the observable universe. This change in perspective from the micro to the macro—from the parts to the whole—is a monumental shift, but it is certainly possible. Just as we can expand our vision in our mind's eye from the Earth to the whole universe, we can also expand our view of ourselves to see our lives in the context of the whole body of life.

Our individualism has enabled us to accomplish amazing things, but valuing unity will take us further. When we view the Earth from outer space, there are no boundaries between countries and people are so small that we are not even visible. Humans are miniscule in the grand scheme of the cosmos, but we have great power to create in the universe. By recognizing what we all have in common—we are all just part of this big blue marble floating through space for starters—we can unify to create and achieve much greater things than we could ever achieve or create individually. We can choose to design a better future together. When we are unified, we have the power to live and create in sustainable ways that support the whole body of life.

We are one

As humans, we appear to be completely separate from each other, other forms of life, and matter—but things are not always as they appear. Absolutely everything comes from a single source of matter and energy that was at one time an integrated whole. The atoms in us today have been in many bodies and things, and they will continue to be used in other bodies and things long after we are gone. This is also true of the energy that animates us. Energy cannot be destroyed, and the life force that energizes us as individuals will energize other living things after we die. Science is making major strides toward finding empirical proof of our connectedness, but even without getting into advanced physics, it is obvious we are not completely separate, discrete individuals.

It is theorized that in the beginning everything was a singularity—perhaps of infinite density and energy and zero mass—and the Big Bang caused a great fragmentation of the whole, setting things in motion. The original oneness inflated out into what we now know as the universe or cosmos. In the process of inflating, all the original matter separated and then joined together again to form stars, planets, moons, comets, galaxies, and everything else in the known universe. On our own planet, life arose, or arrived, and from those first cells came all life—unicellular microorganisms, bacteria, plants, and animals.

Atoms are the chemical building blocks of all organic and inorganic matter. All the atoms that make up everything on Earth were once part of a star—a celestial body outside our solar system. This means that each atom is very, very old. As Carl Sagan wrote in *The Cosmic Connection*: "All of the rocky and metallic material we stand on, the iron in our blood, the calcium in our teeth, the carbon in our genes were produced billions of years ago in the interior of a red giant star. We are made of star-stuff." Various combinations of different atoms create the molecules that make up everything, including the cells in the human body. For example: the human body contains molecules of oxygen, carbon, hydrogen, nitrogen, calcium, phosphorus, potassium, sulfur, chlorine, sodium, and magnesium (and trace amounts of many other elements); the proteins that make up spider silk are made of carbon, hydrogen, oxygen, and nitrogen; the primary chemical components of carbon-manganese steel are carbon, manganese, and iron; and the building blocks of wood are carbon, oxygen, and hydrogen.

Humans are made from atoms that have been cycling and recycling through the universe for billions of years. The atoms in us have been in other organic and inorganic compositions, and when they leave our body they will become part of new bodies and materials. All living beings are constantly taking in and losing atoms. Plants take in carbon and oxygen in the form of carbon dioxide and release oxygen. Every time we inhale we take in atoms of nitrogen, oxygen, argon, and carbon (along with anything else that might be in the atmosphere), and when we exhale we lose carbon, hydrogen, and oxygen atoms. We take in atoms when we eat, and we lose atoms when we expel our waste. We lose skin cells and hair during the course of each day, and we continue losing atoms after we die. Depending on our religion, societal norms, and laws, the atoms in our body will usually be disbursed after death by cremation or decomposition, and used again and again in other living bodies and things.

According to the First Law of Thermodynamics, energy cannot be created or destroyed; it either changes form or is redistributed. When a living body dies, the energy it had is not entirely lost. Our bodies are animated by energy: the sinoatrial node sends electrical impulses to the heart to keep it beating; neurons in the brain produce electrical impulses that regulate and enable everything else a body does. This energy is not destroyed when a body comes to the end of its life. It does not matter if we call this energy a soul, spirit, or life force, or if we believe it is simply the result of physical and chemical reactions. The energy continues on, like a chorus of cosmic vibrations, transferring from one thing to the next in the flow of life.

When two things appear to be completely different, it may seem inconceivable they come from, or are connected to, the same source. However, everything arose from a single source of matter and energy. We are all connected on an atomic level, and whether we realize it or not, we are all part of one body of life.

Oneness and the Collatz conjecture

When we are aware of the oneness and connectedness of all creation, we begin to notice it everywhere. What goes on at the smallest level in life reflects and is connected to what goes on at the universal level of life, and the whole is reflected microcosmically in all its parts. This is nicely illustrated by an atom. It is no coincidence that the electrons circling the nucleus of an atom look like a solar system. An atom is made up of a nucleus and subatomic particles that appear to be separate—atoms are 99.9999% space—but an atom is a single unit. So it is with us and all of creation. Despite the seeming divisions between everything, we are all connected and integral parts of a single whole.

The whole can be seen mathematically with the Collatz conjecture that states we can start with any natural number (positive integer) and get back to one. If the number is even, divide it by two. If the number is odd, multiply it by three and add one. By continuing this process with each resulting number, we eventually return to the number one. The number of times the process is repeated to reach one is the "oneness" of the number. For example, the oneness of three is seven, and it is calculated as follows: 3 x 3 = 9, and 9 + 1 = 10; 10 ÷ 2 = 5; 5 x 3 = 15, and 15 + 1 = 16; 16 ÷ 2 = 8; 8 ÷ 2 = 4; 4 ÷ 2 = 2; and 2 ÷ 2 = 1. There is no way to determine if the Collatz conjecture is true for all natural numbers without running the sequence into infinity, but the probability of it being true is very high.

In a reflection of the connectedness of the universe, the Collatz conjecture shows us that all natural numbers point back to one. The number one is the building block of all natural numbers, and by adding one to itself again and again we get all natural numbers into infinity. One creates many from one, and yet, by using a simple procedure, we can return to the original one—the single, necessary whole that natural numbers depend on for their existence. The number one represents a single set of infinite numbers in the same way oneness, or unity, can represent us as a collective whole and as whole individuals.

Unity consciousness

None of us would be here without the Big Bang—that first great fragmentation of the whole that set things in motion in our universe. Life took hold on Earth and grew strong, and cycles of life and death have been repeating ever since. All living things, with their individual characteristics and uniqueness, will follow the same path back to our source. Death is the inescapable rule of the game of life, and it is that which all living things have in common. However, it is important to recognize that whole ecosystems can perish just as individuals do. Our illusion of separation and isolation from the whole is the cause of pain, disease, stress, and dysfunction spreading through the body of life, and our survival as a species is in jeopardy. This illusion allows us to live in ways that hurt the whole, because we think that damaging something over there is not going to affect us over here. As we are beginning to see, however, this is not the case— many environmental ecosystems, political movements and economies have demonstrated interconnectedness on a global scale. With connections made manifest through new technologies, we can now realize our impact, both positive and negative, at unprecedented speeds.

If we want a healthy future for all life on our planet, we must remember that we are one. We are made of the same stuff—the same atoms, the same chemicals, the same energy throughout the universe. We are all cells in the great body of life called the universe, and we cannot separate ourselves from it. That which damages the whole also damages us.

Now is the time to come together in unity—in unity consciousness—to act together for the benefit of all life. We can take our time, and endure great pain, or we can change our minds now and evolve to a new way of being. The longer we wait to embrace our unity, the longer we will suffer. How much more we will suffer is up to us.

Our awakening from the illusion of separation, and our recognition of our oneness, will signal a distinct new evolutionary phase of humanity. Today we have the opportunity to expand our perspective and our consciousness. When we remember the interconnected nature of all life—when we understand that all life is one—we will begin to be, think, and operate in new ways. Life is beckoning us to do this for our own survival and evolution of consciousness. Together, we can weave the tapestry of life into an amazing masterpiece beyond anything we ever imagined possible.

When we awaken from the illusion of separation we know we are all interconnected and united as one, and we understand that all our actions affect the whole, including us as individuals. The phrase "you get what you give" makes sense in the context of unity consciousness because, if we are all one, our actions actually affect us directly. As previously mentioned, energy is never created or destroyed; it is only transferred. When energy is transferred from one person to another in the form of a good deed, a gap is left in the giver that attracts an equally good deed to take its place. Other people will do good back to that person. When energy is transferred in the form of hatred or greed, a gap of hatred or greed is created, ready to be filled. Another way of looking at it would be to say like attracts like. When we live in unity, with love, compassion, and understanding at the foundation of our actions, we in turn give love, compassion, and understanding back to ourselves. When we work to heal and nurture all life, we are healing and nurturing ourselves.

The good news is that unity will triumph over separation regardless of our understanding and actions. There is a clear pattern and a natural order that all things follow, whether we realize it or not. In fact, unity has already prevailed. All things are already unified as a vast body of life. It was and ever will be. Nothing we do or neglect to do will change this fact. It is just a matter of time before we recognize and realize our unity. That said, we have the ability to shorten or lengthen the time it takes for humanity to awaken to our unity, value it, and match our values to our actions. The longer we choose to take before awakening, the more suffering there will be.

2 COMMUNITY

Because we are one, individuals acting in isolation
are often ineffective.
By joining forces with others, we will realize our full potential.

While unity is life's natural state of being, community must happen by choice. Community means supporting our fundamental unity in all that we do. When we do so, we commune and cooperate with those around us. In community, we choose to honor the connections we have with the unified whole of life. We choose to act for the benefit of all the small communities we are part of—families, local religious centers, towns. We choose to act in community with our state or nation. We choose to act together and in alignment with all of humanity and all of life, including the animals, trees, forests, sea creatures, and all living things.

Separation from the greater whole of life, or a lack of a sense of community with the whole body of life, creates "dis-ease" and illness. People experience this dis-ease on a personal level; for example, studies indicate that certain addictions may be correlated with a sense of isolation and disconnection from others and, similarly, people have greater chances of recovery when they have support networks. Organizations face similar dis-ease when the employees are not valued and treated as integral parts of the organizational system. Nations too feel the dis-ease of isolated action within a global community, or when the citizens do not feel represented by their leaders.

Many people approach life as if they live in bubbles of isolation rather than from a holistic perspective; however, a simple shift in one's thinking can expand such a limited vision to reveal connections everywhere. We are like waves in one ocean of creation—like sunbeams radiating from one sun. By simply reaching out to our neighbors, we realize that we all have shared goals and challenges and if we join forces, we may have all the tools and resources we need already available to us. Sometimes, just by breaking free from our self-limiting viewpoints and experiencing a sense of community and support, that feeling alone is enough to cure ourselves from the diseases of disconnection. With a more holistic perspective that takes into consideration the collective context in which we live, we open the door to the possibility of discovering remedies to our individual, community, and national challenges together.

By building communities, we have the opportunity to share our strengths and overcome our weaknesses. Each person has unique qualities that he or she can bring to a group. One person has special technical skills and another is gifted in artistic expression. One person is a talented mother and another addresses fatherhood in his own unique way. One person grows our food and another delivers it. One person creates the law and another enforces it. One makes us laugh and another touches our hearts to make us cry. One person connects the dots of the work done by others to create an entirely new thing. We recognize in community that by combining our individual strengths we are more powerful than we ever could be alone.

Each person is an individual expression of life itself just as each flower is a unique expression of beauty. When we look at a field of daisies, all of the flowers may all blend into one white sea, but upon closer inspection, each flower has its own characteristics that make it unique. Some may stand up tall, some may bend to the left or to the right. Some may be tattered and others may have slightly different colors. Some are dying and some are just starting to blossom. The beauty of community comes when each individual is a fully actualized expression of himself or herself.

When we remove the blocks within ourselves that limit our capabilities, we allow life to flow through us and actualize the intention of the universe through us. It is as if each of us is an instrument being played by the universe in one song of creation. One can think of humanity as a full symphony composed of string instruments, tubas, trombones, flutes and percussion. Without any one instrument, the complete score could not be fully expressed. Everything plays a fundamental part in the grand symphony of creation, and we are all the instruments of life. For the orchestra to reach its full potential, each individual must be fully expressed in harmony with the other members.

Valuing community means understanding that the various roles we play in our lives affect other people, and the body of life as a whole. It means taking responsibility for our actions, and ensuring that we work for the benefit of all. Every day we make decisions that affect others. When we are aware of this, and choose to act in community, we do our best to make sure that our actions are generally supportive rather than harmful. The choices we make every day range from the smallest kindness on a personal level to major decisions that will affect many people. For example: if we have elderly neighbors we can help them with their shopping or take out their garbage; we can offer our seats on crowded trains and buses to people who need them more than we do; if we have children, we can volunteer to assist at their schools or for after-school programs; if we are civil servants we can go a little bit out of our way to help someone get what they need; if we are lawyers we can do pro bono work; if we are architects and engineers we can design energy efficient, healthy buildings; if we are doctors we can offer free services in times of crisis and disaster. We have the power to make choices every day that support community as a value, and that help us build strong communities and support networks.

Each of our actions and choices affect many individuals and communities. In turn, our communities affect, and are affected by, all the other communities on the planet. To value community is to value the many communities—the many circles of life—around the world. It benefits us all to work together as one integrated system composed of many interdependent parts. When we value community we imagine ourselves in the shoes of people in other communities, and join forces for mutual benefit.

While we are, as individuals, invaluable in and of ourselves—unique expressions of life and part of the whole—we must work as communities if we wish to be truly effective. Together we can overcome individual shortcomings and join strengths as a powerful force for social transformation. When many people take this approach, each community will make choices and take actions that are more sustainable in the context of the whole. In community, we have the opportunity to communicate and work with each other in cooperation, and to live in unity.

The human body as a microcosm of the whole

A human body can be seen as a microcosm of the body of humanity. In a healthy body, all the cells, tissues, and organs work together. When humanity is healthy, individuals, communities, and countries work together. Diseases and illnesses plague our individual bodies as social ills plague the body of humanity. As individuals, we are like cells in the body of humanity, and the potential and abilities of the cells in our bodies are like the potential and abilities that we have vis-à-vis the body of humanity.

When cells stop cooperating with other cells, begin multiplying uncontrollably, and potentially endanger the body they produce cancer. In the macrocosm of humanity, some groups are asserting their strengths to the detriment of the whole—just as cancer cells do in the body. Cancer cells are only a threat when the body is weakened and stressed; they do not survive and thrive in a healthy body with a strong immune system. In the body of humanity, conflicts between apparent opposites are caused by a lack of cooperation and losing sight of the fact that we are one. The threats posed by this lack of cooperation are lessened when we strengthen the body of humanity by joining together as one community.

Like embryonic stem cells that can become any cell in a body, we too are capable of becoming many things. Once the embryonic stem cells differentiate into adult stem cells and all the other cells that make up a body, each cell will have a particular function. After differentiation, adult stem cells can change into particular cells as needed, and every cell still contains the genetic blueprint, the DNA, for the whole. As individuals, we all have the ability and DNA to fulfill many roles, but we often have specific skills and duties assigned to us in this life. Although our families, communities, or societies may guide us into certain roles, we still have the responsibility of ensuring that our roles do not go against our values. We can choose to fulfill this role or that role. We are free to choose whether we work for or against the whole. Young people who live in areas filled with gang violence can follow in the footsteps of their peers and join a gang, or they can choose to take a different path that supports the development of their communities instead. Those who are attracted to terrorist groups can choose to protect their cultures or religious beliefs through violence, or they can choose to be instruments of love and peacefully show the world the richness and beauty of their cultures and religions. The point is that, as individuals, we choose what to make of our lives. If we are not happy with the place we have been guided to, we can go somewhere else. Like embryonic stem cells, we have the ability and DNA to fulfill many roles. No matter where we come from, or where we are, we can all seek ways to work together for the greater good.

Valuing community means working together as one—from all our differing perspectives—for the health of the body of humanity and the body of life. Every human is a unique, differentiated individual with specific strengths and weaknesses. Both the collective body of humanity and the individual human body work most efficiently, and to their fullest potential, when all parts perform their strengths together. Everyone has the chance to shine when individual gifts are combined. The combined strengths compensate for individual weaknesses, and the whole is fortified.

The Golden Rule

The Golden Rule is a maxim based on reciprocity— one should treat others as one would like others to treat oneself. The idea dates from ancient times, and it is a precept found in many cultures and religions. For example, in Islam, "Not one of you truly believes until you wish for others that which you wish for yourself"; in Buddhism, "Hurt not others in ways that you yourself would find hurtful"; in Judaism, "Do unto others as you would have others do unto you"; and in Christianity, "All things whatsoever ye would that men should do to you, do ye so to them; for this is the law and the prophets". When we understand that we are one and choose to live in community, the Golden Rule can serve as the foundation for a new ethics. We refrain from treating others in ways that one would not like to be treated because we understand that doing something to another equates to doing it to oneself. Conversely, taking actions that benefit others also benefit ourselves, and this will ensure that individuals act to the benefit of their communities. When we choose to live by the Golden Rule, we agree to work in partnership with each other, our communities, and the whole.

To date, the Golden Rule has never been successfully implemented on a broad scale. There have always been those who would deviate from this principle, acting only for personal gain and manipulating others for their own benefit. In the face of global terrorism or, on a local level, in an environment of gang violence, it may seem unsafe and unwise to practice the Golden Rule. How can society possibly overcome violence and "us versus them" perspectives to realize the benefits of cooperating as one global community? As stated by Tony Blair, the former Prime Minister of Great Britain and Northern Ireland, in a 2007 essay entitled *A Battle for Global Values*, "[Y]ou cannot defeat a fanatical ideology just by imprisoning or killing its leaders; you have to defeat its ideas. [. . .] We will not win the battle against global extremism unless we win it at the level of values as much as that of force." Although the Prime Minister was not promoting empathy and reciprocity in this statement, he did suggest that a transformation in values is the key to both our safety and security. While the use of force may be appropriate in certain circumstances, we must seek a perceptual shift from divided communities to a more unified, holistic and global approach. By setting the Golden Rule as our standard, we provide a benchmark for appropriate action and a context in which to gauge what is healthy and what is harmful to ourselves, our communities and the world. As an increasing number of people adopt such values, this new perspective has the potential to become the standard view.

Our experiment with separation and isolation has strengthened our character and allowed us to become fully developed as individuals, but our journey does not end there. Nothing lasting can be accomplished in isolation. With courage and determination we can break free from the shackles of our narrow perception of ourselves as separate and isolated individuals to realize our unified and interdependent nature. Grounded in our unity, we then choose to live in community, sharing our talents and skills to be fully expressed version of ourselves. Only together can we realize our full potential.

3 LIFE

Life energizes and moves all things.
The continuity of life is the core of our existence.

Life is a dynamic and powerful force of nature that flows through us and expresses itself in material form. It is the source of all creation, and the energy that sustains and connects all living things. It binds us together in one interconnected and interdependent network of existence. Connected by this common thread, we are part of a global community of living things in which no one form of life, and no individual life, is more inherently valuable than another. All things are part of this web of life. What affects one form of life affects all forms of life; all parts impact the whole. As such, all life is an integral part of a complex system and therefore precious—the life of the planet, the life of the environment, the microbial life, the plant life, and the animal life, including humans. Together, all living things make up one body of life.

Life is the vehicle that carries and expresses the infinite intelligence of the universe on its journey through space and time. We often think we are living our lives, but it is really the other way around. Life animates us, flows through us, and expresses itself through us. Life is like a warm breeze traveling through time experiencing all it can experience—states of being, physical sensations, the full spectrum of emotions. We are merely conduits for the expression of life itself, and we are being lived by a force much greater than we can imagine.

Life is not to be claimed and conquered. It is to be shared and transferred from one thing to the next like an eternal gift which is passed on through the generations.

The grand flow of life

The world is alive and electric with the vibrations of life. There is life energy all around us, animating us, connecting us, running through us, and continuing its journey. Life circulates from one body to the next, from one living thing to the next, in a continuous flow.

When we look around we see plants growing, birds flying, spiders spinning, animals playing, and people bustling by. If we stop and listen we hear the whispers of the wind, the calls of animals and insects, people's voices, and the whirring of things that humans have created—engines, fans, computers, mobile phones, household appliances, industrial machinery. All these things, whether they sprang forth directly from nature or were created by us, collectively vibrate with energy. This energy is transferred from one thing to the next in a river of creation.

The flow of life can be seen in the movement of nature. A seed is supported by soil and water, and begins to take root. As it grows, sprigs and shoots erupt from the soil and enable the new plant to harness the energy of the sun through photosynthesis. This energy is necessary for the plant to grow or flower or bear fruit. When the plant or its fruit is consumed, life is transferred and continues its journey through another living thing. The seeds of the new plant are spread around by animals after consumption, by the wind, or in other ways, and the cycle begins again. This continual transfer of life from one thing to the next—the cycle of life, death, and life—is essential for future generations of the plant, and other living things that rely on the plant for sustenance.

We are all given the gift of life when we are born. We pass on this gift when we have children, serve others, and create things that support and nurture life as a whole. After life has finished its journey through us, we die but the energy that we have transferred to our children, our loved ones, and our creations is carried on through them. As our bodies are returned to ash or clay the energy they held is transferred to other forms of life.

Change is life's great constant. Everything is always in flux—becoming, existing, creating, transitioning, and dying. We live in and among and through continuing cycles of creation and destruction reflected in our bodies, our families, our communities, our countries. Life creates, bursts forth, blooms, reproduces, and dies to make way for new life. Landscapes are shaped by blowing wind, flowing water, lightning strikes, earthquakes, floods, wildfires, and when something is swept away in destruction life quickly moves in to replace what was lost with new life. The energy of life is merely transferred from one thing to another in a continuous stream of movement within the whole of creation. This journey—this flow, movement, transformation, creation, destruction, and continuation of life—is the essence of life itself.

The evolution of self-awareness and consciousness

Life is the spirit that moves us in this playground of matter. Although the continuous transfer of life energy is essential, it is not the only purpose, or function, of life. As life energy is transferred from one thing to the next it carries with it a great intelligence and consciousness. In a miracle of creation, life animates matter, and it drives all living things to evolve. Our ultimate purpose, and the ultimate purpose of life itself, is the evolution of consciousness and self-awareness.

In the beginning, a fundamental force or will created all that is in our world. This force has been described in many ways and by many names—God, Nature, Source, or simply Life itself. Regardless of what name or characteristics we give this force, it animates the world through vibration giving material things life. An initial burst of energy spread out through the universe humming the song of creation. All things, including rocks and leaves and even furniture or appliances resonate with a vibration of the universe. Unlike such seemingly inanimate objects or even other animals, we humans have evolved to have the capacity for self-awareness and introspection. We have the ability to reflect on ourselves and realize our impact on our surroundings.

Through our self-awareness, life and the consciousness that it carries embraces the opportunity to express and know itself through our intellectual reflection and self-realization. In this game of self-discovery we have come to realize our source, and we understand that just as life created us, we also create life—and we have a role to play in its evolution. Rather than living a constricted and limited life of oneself, one's family, one's community, or one's nation, we can join with all life in the world and the universe. Instead of merely living our life, we can choose to be lived *by* life consciously. We can assist something much greater than us to actualize its destiny through us.

When we are lived by life we consciously choose to push ourselves toward greater self-awareness, and we live in harmony with, and with respect for, all of creation because we recognize that we are intimately connected to all of creation. As we begin to match our individual will with our value of life we ultimately break free from our illusion of isolation and separation. We realize the continuity of all things, and that we have always been free and connected to all things by the force of life. When life lives us, everything—the things we create and build, the money we acquire, the children we have, the possessions we maintain—becomes an integral component of the evolution of consciousness itself.

As self-aware beings we manifest our will by directing our intentions, energies, and actions toward an end. We can choose to manifest our will in ways that support life, or in ways that hinder life and support death. When we value life we choose to nurture it, and we use our intentions and energies to co-create with the source of our being. In doing this, we give meaning to our individual lives, and we support the body of life as a whole. In a way, we are liberated from our smaller selves to see ourselves as part of all of creation; we become instruments of life itself, and we can join the hand of creation. When we align our interests with the life force of the universe we will evolve to our highest potential. This is our destiny. This is why we are here. This is the purpose of life.

FREEDOM

Freedom is a natural right.
Democratic principles are the foundation of social justice.

Freedom of will lies at the heart of the human experience. Through our will, we create our world and unless we exercise our will, we are not free. Our ability to think as conscious, volitional individuals empowers us to manifest our will within the world and to make choices that reflect our values. Such freedom of the mind is essential for people to fully participate in society as citizens and collectively as communities, states, and nations.

When we choose to enact our free will—and claim our inherent freedom of consciousness—we have the power to shape the world. By matching our actions to our values, we are free to will our lives into being whatever we wish them to be. It is by virtue of our freedom that we have the opportunity to be master-masons of life, and to create the life we choose. Freedom is the foundation of human creation. Only by exercising our capacity to think and choose, can we further create social and political structures that reflect our value of freedom.

By valuing freedom for ourselves and for others, we take a stand for many individual and collective rights including—freedom of speech, freedom of the press, freedom of association, and freedom of religion. Freedom of expression is one of the most fundamental aspects of all forms of freedom. With freedom of expression, people are afforded the opportunity to express what they think is right and wrong and to provide alternative ideas. When people are free to express their ideas without fear of retaliation, their creativity can be expressed for the benefit of everyone.

When we recognize that we are all connected as one body of life, valuing freedom means valuing freedom for all rather than just our individual selves. It means respecting that all people have the right to think and express themselves and thereby manifest their individual will. When we choose to use our freedom to embrace values and take actions that benefit and support the greater whole, we facilitate the fullest form of expression of life through individuals and collectively as a society. In doing so, we can reach beyond ourselves to affect the lives of others and gain from their creative contributions to society and the many diverse viewpoints expressed.

Individual freedom

Each day we are presented with many options, and we make many choices. We make choices in our personal life, and we make choices in our public life. Although we are born with free will, it is our freedom—or the extent to which we are free—that mostly determines the type and number of choices available to us. In general, the freer we are, the more choices we have.

Freedom on a personal level is something most of us have and exercise each day without giving it a second thought. We decide to eat this rather than that. We choose to say one thing over another. We choose to turn left instead of right. Relatively speaking, few of us are limited to the extent that we cannot exercise our individual freedom at this level.

Individual freedom within the public sphere, and in relation to others, operates a bit differently. The freedom we are granted in our societies is a function of collective agreements. For an agreement to hold, at least two parties must consent to be governed by it. If consent is not given, the agreement may be amended or perhaps discarded and never manifest. The point is that these agreements are subject to change, depending on the agreements among the members of the society. If a society agrees that its citizens should be free, so it is. People will work to enact rules and legislation that protect those freedoms. If a society agrees that its citizens should not be free, so it is. People will create social structures that restrict the freedoms of certain groups. If a society agrees that one small group shall dictate the destiny of all, so it is. People will abdicate their freedom to a select few, and allow them to rule over the majority. If a society agrees to implement democracy, so it is. People will adopt a constitution that protects the rights of all members of society. In the same way, interpersonal agreements create the context in which, and the rules by which, we act with and toward others in our personal dealings. We learn that we must respect the boundaries—stated or otherwise—we have with others if we wish to maintain harmonious relationships with them. If we choose to act in ways that go against any of our collective agreements we may find ourselves in arguments, personal disputes, legal challenges, or even jail.

In today's world, many of us do not give much thought to the collective agreements that inform our individual freedom. This means that our consent is often given by default. It may be argued that whole societies do not typically agree to be ruled by a dictator, or to live under the boot of fascism. However, inaction in these situations—when we choose to live within the boundaries that are set by the societal collective agreement—effectively equates to consent.

Freedom requires great responsibility, and many of us are afraid of taking this responsibility. Sometimes we knowingly give away our power to rule ourselves in the hopes that others with more experience will make better decisions for us because we are scared to make our own mistakes. As a result, we can wake up one day only to find ourselves going along with things we do not truly support or believe in or consent to. As long as our situation is not too uncomfortable we stick with our apathy and our consent remains in place, or sometimes we might choose not to withdraw our consent out of fear—fear for our lives, fear of change, fear we do not have the capacity to make good decisions, fear of making mistakes. However, when we dare to claim our power, the responsibility for our future success or failure shifts squarely on to us, and that is a wonderful responsibility to have.

When we claim our power we can no longer blame others for our failures, but we can exercise our free will to make the life we want. Taking responsibility for our power and actions allows us to learn from our mistakes and failures, and to adapt and change to ensure future success. When we claim our power, the future lies in our hands and that is the core of freedom.

In unfree systems, the spark of individual freedom is risky. However, when even one person dares to claim his or her individual freedom as a fundamental power, then that person starts a fire within the whole that shines brighter than any collective malaise. That one person has the potential to awaken others to the possibility of change. By working together with other citizens, new collective agreements can be forged, and new societal freedoms can arise. That is known as revolution.

We are ultimately free to build the lives and societies that we choose. At the most base level, we are free to harm or to help others—we can choose to support our individual lives and societies at the expense of others, or we can choose to support the greater whole of humanity and all societies. We make the best use of our freedom when we choose to exercise our individual freedom for the benefit of all. In doing so, we are aligning ourselves with the creative force of life itself.

Democracy and freedom

Freedom is an open door to all who wish to walk through it. Unfortunately, some people charge through the door and assert their freedom at the expense of others, and some of us will sit back quietly and watch—despite the costs of losing our own freedom in the process. For this reason, when we truly value freedom and social justice, we must also value democracy. Democracy is the political system most conducive to allowing for the protection of the well-being, vitality, and life of humanity and the greater whole. Authentic democracy upholds freedom, equality of rights, and opportunities for all people, and it works to ensure such opportunities are secured for future generations. It is the arm of justice that prevents individuals from using their own personal freedom to control and overpower others. Democratic principles are the foundation of social justice.

The word democracy comes from the Greek *dēmokratia*, meaning "people power," or the "rule of the people." Democracy is the political system best equipped to protect the freedom of all because it recognizes and accepts that power lies with the people. The power of the people is at the heart of democracy, and democracy functions best with the involvement of all.

Citizens in democracies have the great responsibility of participating in their governments by exercising their voting rights. In the days of the ancient Greeks, during the advent of Athenian democracy in the fifth century B.C., citizens of the Greek city-state (known as a polis) of Athens debated and made decisions over the destiny of the polis at the Greek market, called the Agora. The Agora served as the center of artistic, athletic, and political life and as well as philosophical discourse, a place where one might hear arguments by the likes of Socrates and Plato echoing in the streets. In the Agora, however, only men, who were citizens of the polis, were allowed to participate in these discussions and to vote on legislation and executive bills. Since ancient Greek times, the concept of democracy has evolved to be much more inclusive of all people. Today, women have the right to vote in all Western and most Eastern societies. Further, non-citizens of European Union countries are permitted to vote at local elections in a fellow European Union country where they are permanently living.

Unfortunately, many people often fail to use their voting rights, because they do not believe their vote makes a difference, are apathetic or are just disappointed by the system. When we all take this responsibility to heart—when we all vote and actively engage in other democratic processes—the interests that will benefit the whole come to the fore and are protected. As Aristotle wrote: "If liberty and equality, as is thought by some, are chiefly to be found in democracy, they will be best attained when all persons alike share in the government to the utmost."

A truly democratic system ensures that power lies with all the people, rather than with a select few. It enables all to speak their truths through freedom of expression, while safeguarding that the principles incorporated into our social fabric benefit the majority in the long term, if not the whole. All individuals can make their voices heard, but the majority will determine that which is best for all. In this way, anything that does not support the benefit of the majority will not be included in the collective agreement. Unfortunately, there are many so-called democratic countries where censorship and other means of suppressing freedom of expression exist. States or other groups in power may pass laws to prevent freedom of speech and freedom of the press, making it illegal for people to express criticism of those in power and their policies. Such censorship and suppression of self-expression act to inhibit the basic freedoms of the people.

Democratic principles are the rules and guidelines through which we can secure equality, protections, and social justice for every individual playing this game of life. They allow for diverse interests to be fairly represented while providing fundamental rights, protections, limitations on power, and recourse. Some basic principles include: human rights; control of the abuse of power; equality; political tolerance; bill of rights; economic freedom; citizen participation; accountability; transparency; a multi-party system; regular free and fair elections; and due process of law. These principles level the playing field. They create space for all the players on the team, and they give rules by which all the players must abide. A political system that operates under democratic principles is the way to ensure equality of opportunity and freedom for humanity.

Freedom is our birthright. It is up to us to claim it. Freedom rings through the vibrations of the eternal bell of righteousness that tolls for all who seek justice in this world. It is the glorious sound that resonates with all people. As Dr. Martin Luther King, Jr. proclaimed in his *I Have A Dream* speech: "Let freedom ring....From every mountainside, let freedom ring."

5 CONNECTION

*All things have a profound impact on each other—
global economies, cultures, environments, political systems,
and our minds, bodies, and spirits.*

Much of the suffering we experience today is caused by a profound sense of disconnection permeating our societies and our lives. Our isolationist paradigm encourages myopic, individualist viewpoints, rather than an elevated, inclusive view of our connection to the whole. When we believe we are alone and disconnected from the world, we tend to live independent and compartmentalized lives. We isolate ourselves in little houses, offices, and work cubicles. We live in large apartment buildings that house hundreds of people, yet many of us do not even know our closest neighbors. We listen to music on headphones so that we do not have to listen to other peoples' conversations or engage in conversation ourselves. We do everything we can to create safe and comfortable spaces for ourselves—often by blocking ourselves off from the rest of the world. In other words, we come to believe that our personal safety and comfort rely on disconnection and isolation from the whole.

In addition to producing a sense of disconnection from each other, our faulty thinking has also lead many of us to become disconnected from the global challenges we face. Everywhere we look, things are falling apart: economies and governments are collapsing; fuel and food prices are soaring; and our energy sources threaten our safety. Yet, many of us try to act as if everything is fine, and avoid such troubling topics. We have polite, surface interactions, and our daily conversations are usually limited to routine exchanges. We throw ourselves into our fast-paced lives so we do not have time to worry as we run from here to there multitasking. Understandably, many people also try to cut themselves off from reality by numbing themselves with alcohol, drugs, television, and movies. In our suffering, we do anything we can to tune out the world.

The reality is that our sense of disconnection is an illusion. We are not alone, and we are not isolated from the rest of the world, no matter how hard we try to block ourselves off from others. All things affect each other: environments, ecosystems, political systems, societies, cultures, economies, mind, body, spirit, soul, and self. In the same way that a message in a bottle dropped in the sea can be carried thousands of miles on the tides, all the thoughts and actions of each individual living thing directly affect the whole as they are carried out into the sea of consciousness.

When we all act from narrow viewpoints—and only for our own benefit—we function in unhealthy competition with each other rather than in cooperation, both as societies and individuals. Such competition at the expense of the whole often leads to disharmony, disease, death, and destruction. Today's reality is that we no longer have the luxury, or sufficient natural resources, to sustain such isolationist viewpoints and actions. We are facing crises that threaten the very existence of humanity on this planet. If we hope to survive on Earth, we need a holistic paradigm that values and supports the inherent connection of all life and cooperation among its many members.

As technology shrinks the world, our connectedness becomes more apparent and action taken against the greater good becomes increasingly untenable. Disconnection leads to isolation and fear, and as we act to protect ourselves out of fear we produce more separation, isolation, and disconnection. Connection, on the other hand, produces love, and an attitude of love connects us to others. Just as we can choose to live in disconnection and fear, so too can we choose to live in connection and love. The choice is ours.

By joining forces, we gain power in the face of crisis.

Despite the clear need for mass collective action on the issues facing humanity, our societal responses are often as disconnected from reality as our individual responses. In fact, in dealing with a crisis, our societal action is often the polar opposite of that which could possibly remedy the situation. We are in economic crisis, but we continue to print more money. Ice caps, glaciers, permafrost, and tundra are melting, but we continue to emit greenhouse gases and use more and more technologies that heat up the planet. Fossil fuels are running out, but we fail to implement new, cleaner sources of energy. We cut costs at the expense of health and safety. We are killing our bees—without which the chain of life on Earth will collapse—yet we continue to spray our crops with pesticides, and carry on as if what poisons other forms of life will not eventually poison us. The list goes on and on....

We seem to be waiting for our leaders to fix all these things for us, but they are so invested in the status quo that they repeatedly fail to address our problems with any great success. It may feel like we are the victims here, but this is not the case. Our societies and ways of interacting reflect our beliefs and our collective agreements. As such, everything is not happening *to* us; it is happening *because* of us. While an isolationist paradigm can have great individual benefits, it does not answer our inherent need to live in connection with others. This mismatch between the prevailing worldview and our essential nature has produced social structures that do not reflect our needs. This combined with a lack of awareness of our part in permitting such practices results in us feeling like vulnerable victims. However, when we understand we can adopt a different perspective and change our beliefs, modes of being, and modes of operating, we realize that we are not all doomed to victimhood. Together we are strong and can reclaim our individual and collective power to create better societies and lives.

Sometimes it can seem like people are so ensconced in their own myopic worldviews based on separation and isolation that there is no hope of individuals ever joining together for the greater good. Fortunately, reality proves otherwise. However painful it is to see people dying and suffering in a natural disaster, we can take heart from the inevitable human response that always follows such an occurrence. Whether it is a tsunami in Japan, an earthquake in Haiti or Nepal, a wildfire in Colombia, or a hurricane in New York, many people always step up to the plate to help others in life-and-death situations. People from unaffected parts of the community, other communities, and even other parts of the world are prompted to act—directly on the ground, or by giving material or financial support—on behalf of those in distress. It is of no import that relief efforts are usually temporary, or that feelings of camaraderie and love for our fellow humans can be short-lived and not reach beyond those in immediate need. What is significant is that we remember that we have the capacity to have empathy for, and to act on behalf of, others. If we can do it once, we can do it again and again. This is the important thing to understand. When we join together in the service of others, and for the greater good, we act in alignment with and support of, life, and we shine as humanity.

Where do we start reclaiming our connection to all that is?

We start with ourselves. We start by changing our minds and taking a holistic perspective. Our thoughts affect everything we feel, do, and create. When we choose to make a shift in our thinking we begin to think new thoughts, take new actions, and operate in new ways. As we do these things we create new patterns and practices that reflect our recognition of the whole, which in turn reinforces our new way of being and our connection to all that is.

It is not always easy to see how our own thoughts affect everything, but with a little effort we can usually see that this is indeed true. If, for example, we set out to have a good day, chances are things will at least go a bit more smoothly than if we go about our business looking for a fight. If we approach a new experience thinking we will definitely not like it, then we will probably end up having a bad time; if we go with an open mind, we have a much better chance of appreciating the new experience. If we think we cannot do something, then it is highly doubtful we will even try to do it. On the other hand, if we think we can do something we are free to explore how we might go about doing it, and we could just be pleasantly surprised with the results.

The relationship between thoughts and everything else is much easier to see in others. Most of us have experienced the spoiling of a social occasion or family gathering because of someone else's bad attitude or behavior. If someone is unhappy being somewhere, or with certain people, that person can choose to go with the flow and make the best of it, or not. If someone decides that his or her individual preferences or contentment or desire to complain is more important than respecting the others and the occasion, then that person's presence will usually put a dampener on the affair to one extent or another. We have all witnessed this sort of behavior, whether it was a teenager sulking at the dinner table, an uncle complaining about anything and everything because he wanted to go to the game rather than the wedding, or the friend determined to make a meal miserable for everyone because she did not want to eat at that restaurant. The thoughts and attitudes we bring to every situation put their associated vibrations into the equation, and these vibrations necessarily affect the whole.

By remembering that we are all one we change the way we think and the things we think, and this in turn changes everything around us. When we feel separated from the whole we do not think about how our actions affect others or the environment, or maybe we believe that our actions do not have the potential to affect anything beyond our own lives. However, when we choose to remember our connection to all that is, our perspective shifts. We see everything in a new light. We realize that what we think and do does matter, and that we have a responsibility to protect and preserve the whole as much as we have the same responsibility to ourselves.

This change in perspective translates into new actions because we now understand that our isolationist paradigm and past actions were detrimental to the whole. Perhaps we were never in the habit of turning off lights as we left a room, but now we think about all the costs—resources, energy, pollution—of generating electricity and getting it to all our homes and businesses. As a result, we make sure to turn off lights and appliances when they are not in use. We might recycle or bike to work instead of driving. We might simply try to see the other person's perspective in an argument, and act with compassion rather than anger and defensiveness. These are only small, individual examples of how things can change when we realize the profound impact that all things have on each other and decide to shift our thinking toward a holistic perspective. When everyone makes this shift to value our connection, the changes will be monumental and they will reach far beyond our individual lives.

When we change the way we think, we actually create new biological connections in the brain. Everything that goes on inside our body—all our thoughts, feelings, memories, the functioning of our involuntary nervous system—and everything we do outwardly, requires brain activity. Our brains are made of specialized nerve cells called neurons, and at the most basic level, neural activity means that neurons are firing off electrical signals. These signals carry messages and cause the neurons to release chemical neurotransmitters into the gaps between neurons called synapses. In a process called neurotransmission, other neurons take-up the neurotransmitters (and the messages) from the synapses and pass along the messages (via neurotransmitters) to other neurons. This process of neurons receiving and transmitting messages is repeated again and again as the messages are passed along from neuron to neuron over neural pathways and networks to wherever they need to go. In short, whenever we do something it involves our neurons firing off messages across neural pathways and networks.

We are not born with all the neural pathways we will ever have. Neural pathways are created as we grow and learn, when we change, as a result of behavior, or to compensate for some lost functionality if we have suffered some trauma. The more we do something, the stronger the neural pathways associated with it become, and the more likely we are to repeat this same behavior in the future. This ability of our brain to change—to build new neural pathways—is referred to as neuroplasticity. For example, a person who has suffered a stroke can retrain his or her brain to function effectively by building such new pathways through cognitive and behavioral exercises. Every time we think or do something new our neurons send new messages, and if we continue to think or do this new thing we will eventually create completely new neural pathways associated with it. Hence, as we direct our thoughts and actions into new avenues we literally build those new avenues inside us and rewire our brain. The more we take those new avenues the stronger the neural pathways become, and the stronger the tendency to go down the new avenues again and again.

Some of the neural pathways that have been established in our brains may not serve the highest good for either ourselves or humanity. Addictions, for example, may prompt people to take actions of compulsive and unhealthy dependent behavior. While we may think of addictions in the context of alcohol, drugs, gambling, or sex, our brains can also become addicted to things such as technology, including email, texting, chatting, social media, surfing the Web and video games. While there are certainly benefits to our technological advancements, over consumption may prove to be detrimental, creating neural pathways that reflect unhealthy compulsive behavior. For example, researchers are currently studying the effect of media violence on the brain and whether overexposure to such stimulation may trigger anger responses in the brain.

Neuroplasticity of the brain allows us to change our natural impulses and neural connections to better align with healthy and sustainable practices for ourselves and the world. We can start rebuilding our connection to the whole by shifting our thinking to a holistic perspective. By simply deciding to change our mind we can remember and relearn who we really are—connected and one with all that is. By choosing to recognize that we are one, all of our thoughts, emotions, actions, and creations are underpinned by our connection to the whole. Our intention to live in connection with all of life will automatically reprogram our brain. That is the beauty and miracle of the human body—as we change our minds, our minds physically change. When we think new thoughts we do things in new ways, we rewire our brains, and we can create new lives.

People all around the world are waking up to realize their connection to all that is. Like rare flowers blossoming in isolation in various parts of the world—one person realizes it in Dhaka, another in Des Moines, another in Moscow, another in São Paulo, another in Baghdad, another in Beijing, another in Auckland, and then one in Amsterdam. These people start the process of reprogramming human consciousness. Together, we can change governments, laws, and international policies to support the whole of life. Social institutions and structures are merely reflections of the collective social mindset, and as such, change must begin with each of us individually. As we form a critical mass of individuals who adopt a new, holistic paradigm, we can begin to project a new vision and life-supporting values on a larger scale.

Globalization and connectedness

Today, it is easy to see that we are all connected at the global level. The technological advances that have made it feasible to grow or manufacture something in one hemisphere and sell it in another have led to enormous societal changes. In less than a lifetime, we have seen full-scale globalization in terms of: communications; resources; agriculture; manufacturing; transportation; services; travel; cultural production; and economies. Like the neural pathways that we create in the brain, new global connections provide access to new ways of behavior and interaction. Electronic communications and online functionality have changed the ways we do business, politics, education, art, culture, and religion, as well as the ways we socialize. The connectedness we get as individuals from the Internet, the World Wide Web, email, and social media is one of the greatest goods of globalization. This electronic connectedness is a real-life manifestation of the true connectedness of humanity and all life. However, creating these connections is only part of our journey. By operating under an isolationist paradigm in a connected world, competition has taken priority over collaboration, and the value of short-term profits has risen above the need for long-term sustainability. In order to reap the benefits of globalization, we need to act in accordance with a holistic paradigm that reflects values that support a healthy and sustainable world.

Under an isolationist paradigm, globalization is imbalanced. What it gives with one hand it often takes away with the other. Global markets have opened up, and new markets have been created. While these developments may not always be welcomed, they can be beneficial. We can sell our products, services, art, cars, houses, and just about anything else imaginable to anyone with Internet access. On the other hand, the global marketplace is increasingly dominated by large players. It is becoming harder for individuals to get a foothold, and the risk of becoming a target of a financial crime or identity theft seems to be on the rise. Additionally, when jobs are created in one place, they are often lost from another place. Agriculture subsidies in one country can be a boon to its farmers, but the flooded market in another country can drive local farmers into ruin. Low-cost—and not so low-cost—consumer products often come with long hours and low pay for the workers who manufacture the products, and lack of environmental and health and safety regulations around production. For all the major benefits of globalization, we cannot overlook the fact that it remains yet to be implemented and used for the best advantage of all.

The Internet, the World Wide Web, email, and social media have brought about a revolution in the ways we live our lives. These technologies provide instant access to information and to each other. To an extent, they have liberated us from our physical locations. Our lives now function in a global context, and even if we live in small towns or remote places the world is at our fingertips. Thanks to globalization, and these technologies in particular, we are no longer limited to working, experiencing, buying, or engaging only with that which is local. We can keep in touch with our families and loved ones regardless of physical distance. We can access food, electronics, consumer items, entertainment, data, and even healthcare from many countries. Without leaving our offices, we can work on projects on the other side of the world or across town. In ways that were unimaginable a hundred years ago, our lives are increasingly connected to, and dependent upon, all manner of things in other places.

We are all potentially electronically connected to anyone and everyone on Earth. With the click of a mouse or the touch of a screen we can enter an electronic universe of people, knowledge, stories, creations, and experiences. We see that people everywhere have the same joys, worries, and desires as we do, and that people are genuinely concerned about the well-being of others. We have the opportunity to use these new tools for connection to reflect positive values rooted in a holistic paradigm. Every day, via crowdfunding and online fundraising, people across the world give money to strangers to help them deal with tragedies and disasters, access medical and legal services, provide for other needs, and even start new businesses. People offer heartfelt words of love, comfort, advice, and encouragement for those suffering and in pain through social media. Never before have we been able to directly connect with and support so many others, nor have we been able to witness such regular outpourings of love, compassion, and support for total strangers. When we connect electronically with individuals from across the planet we see our humanity reflected in them, and our own humanity is called forth in connection, compassion, understanding, and support. This is our strength as humans.

Our survival depends on finding a way out of the prevailing isolationist paradigm, and working together to ensure that the planet remains habitable for all life. If we are to be better than parasites dooming our host—and ourselves—we must live and operate in connection with all of creation. Today, we are a global village, and we have the ability to connect with others anywhere in the world to accomplish shared goals. Technology connects us, and this connectedness shows us our natural state of being—it is a reflection of the connectedness of the body of humanity, and the whole body of life. When we live in connection, we join together so we can evolve into a holistic paradigm, and a way of life that is good for the whole.

We are not isolated islands of biology acting alone. All things are connected through the vibrations of energy that circulate through every living thing. As we participate in the grand machinery of the universe these vibrations—this life force—flow through us and connect us to all life. We are partners with all that surrounds us. When we realize our connection, our islands of isolation will disappear into the ocean of all that is. We will live in collaboration as an integrated whole. We will return to our unity and oneness that is, was, and ever shall be. Then, and only then, will we reach our full potential as human beings.

6 SUSTAINABILITY

Sustainable practices are essential to maintain the flow of life for the individual, the community, and the world.

When we think about sustainability, the first thing that comes to mind may be environmental sustainability. This important issue is attracting increased attention in light of the effects of climate change, the depletion of natural resources, and environmental degradation. Environmental sustainability also gets much-deserved attention because of our continued reliance on fossil fuels. Rather than developing clean and renewable energy—wind, solar, and wave, for example—we are using increasingly destructive ways to extract finite fossil fuels from the Earth.

While environmental sustainability is certainly imperative and necessary for our survival, understanding sustainability only in this way provides a very limited view of our predicament. A more complete view of sustainability is holistic, systemic, and global and in order to achieve such a state, we will have to transition into whole new ways of life.

We will need to shift our values from short-term, individual gain at the expense of the whole to long-term, sustainable life for all. When we place our value of sustainability at the heart of all we do, environmental sustainability will automatically follow.

We live in an increasingly demanding and fast-paced world, and it is easy to ignore the issue of sustainability. It is very challenging to get our heads around all the difficulties we face in this area, and it is also hard to see how small changes we could make as individuals might make a real difference for the world. We might find ourselves asking questions such as: What can I possibly do? Will buying recycled paper products really combat deforestation? If I ride my bike to work, will that help to ease the energy crisis? Does it matter if I bring my own shopping bags instead of taking bags from the store? We all know that making small, personal lifestyle changes will not solve any of our crises overnight. So we may become impatient, or consciously opt not to alter our actions because we feel our individual efforts are useless. Or perhaps we feel guilty when we are reminded of the necessity of sustainability, but because we are overwhelmed by the immense scope of the issues involved, we find it easier just to continue in our old ways. We would like to live in a green, glorious world, but it just seems too far out of reach, so we do nothing to achieve it.

Regardless of how we feel about sustainability, or how we choose to live, the fact remains that our actions are destroying the world. Actions based on the egoic belief that we are isolated beings disconnected from others and our environment are unsustainable because they do not take into account the greater whole of life of which we are a part. The ego is the part of us that seeks to defend and glorify the separate and separated self, which works for separation, unhealthy autonomy, and independence. When we act in egoic, individualistic ways at the expense of others, we are like cancer cells ravaging the body of life. If we do not shift into sustainability and change our ways we will ultimately kill ourselves just as cancer cells kill their host.

Given the enormity of the changes required to transition into sustainability, it is no wonder we have not yet managed to correct our unsustainable practices. The good news is that we *can* do it. We will achieve true sustainability when we replace our isolationist paradigm with a holistic one, and replace unsustainable practices with sustainable practices across the board. When we make sustainability a core value, we will work to make everything we do collectively sustainable—energy production, agriculture, urban planning, waste management, research and development, healthcare, education, business, politics, religion, etc.—and sustainability will infuse our interpersonal relations and individual actions. As individuals, rather than dreaming of an idyllic paradise that we believe can never be, we will choose to take small actions—and make choices in each moment—that support all life, each other, and our planet. Doing this as lone, isolated individuals will not deliver all the changes we want, but as more and more of us commit to these small actions, things will begin to change for the better. Then, our institutions, social structures, and laws will begin to change to reflect this new holistic paradigm.

We can continue to suffer, or we can choose sustainable practices that encourage life on Earth to flourish. We can affirm and support all life with holistic practices that nurture the spirit and vitality of ourselves and our environment. In this way, we can create the possibility of working in cooperation with each other and our surroundings to evolve into sustainable ways of life for the benefit of all.

Moving beyond Darwinian survival of the fittest

For most of human history, it was not questioned that cooperation was absolutely necessary for our survival. Our earliest societies were nomadic bands, clans, and tribes that acted together to find shelter, food, and safety. We know from prehistoric cave paintings that hunting was often a collective effort, particularly when the prey was large. In other words, we pulled together to ensure the survival of the group. As societies evolved our groupings became larger, and technology allowed us to achieve more with the cooperation of fewer individuals. Eventually, our cooperative ways were usurped by a fierce sense of individualism, and we lost sight of working for the good of whole. This was facilitated in no small part by the theory of evolution put forward by Charles Darwin.

Theories of evolution existed before Darwin, but it was the publication of his book—*On the Origin of Species by Means of Natural Selection, or the Preservation of Favoured Races in the Struggle for Life*—in 1859 that catapulted the theory of evolution into popular consciousness. Given the second half of the book's title, it is not surprising that Darwin and evolution became associated with the phrase "survival of the fittest" (although it should be noted that Herbert Spencer came up with the phrase). The point is that for well over a century we took it for granted that evolution is the result of survival of the fittest, with the fittest being the strongest, most aggressive, most violent, and most selfish. Coupling this with our survival instincts, and individual fight or flight stress responses, gives us the perfect recipe to justify our isolationist paradigm insofar as it often appears that individuals are only ever concerned with their own survival.

Today, the study of evolution has evolved itself to be more of a cooperative model. Now, the term "the fittest" does not in fact equate to the strongest, most aggressive, most violent, most selfish individuals acting only for their own benefit. Successful species—those that reproduce and secure future generations—possess many traits and display many behaviors that are counter to the Darwinian understanding of survival of the fittest. It is now understood that cooperation and cooperative behaviors are integral to successful species.

We see such cooperation in action in insect colonies. For example, highly social insect groups such as ant and bee colonies operate as unified superorganisms. The individuals in those colonies exist and work in total cooperation, and the colony as a whole functions as a single individual. Significantly, cooperation is not only observed within species, but also between species. For example, cleaner fish cooperate with larger species—even predators—to create symbiotic relationships that benefit both species. Yellow tang fish clean sea turtles, and they get a meal for their trouble. Remora, or suckerfish, earn their dinner by cleaning sharks, rays, and other large marine animals of parasites and other detritus. In the case of the sharks, they could easily eat the remora themselves, but the sharks patiently open their mouths and flare their gills as the cleaner fish dart in and out of their mouths to do the job.

Allegorically, inter-species cooperation is nicely represented in Aesop's fable *The Lion and the Mouse*. A little mouse came across a sleeping lion and began running all over him. This woke the lion, and he trapped the little mouse with his paw. The mouse asked the lion to spare his life, and he said he might be able to help the lion one day. The lion laughed, but he was so amused that he agreed to let the little mouse go. Sometime later, the lion was caught by hunters and tied to a tree. The little mouse was passing by; he saw the trapped lion, and he gnawed through the ropes to set the lion free. The moral of this story is that little friends may prove to be great friends, but as a lesson, the suggestion of inter-species cooperation should not be overlooked.

Today, our very survival as a species is under threat. Our isolationist paradigm encourages and promotes individualistic actions that are destroying us and our environment. This is not sustainable. If we hope to survive, we have to overcome our Darwinian understanding of survival of the fittest and push our evolution forward. When we cooperate with the whole of life, we can transform into a new, sustainable state of being that actively protects and promotes the whole.

How do we transition into a collaborative synthesis?

To begin, we must acknowledge that our current ways of life threaten our very existence. Once we accept this, there is no longer any room to deny that sustainability must be woven into the fabric of our future—because we will have no future without it. By placing our value of sustainability at the heart of all we do, we will bring our actions in line with our intentions to support the whole of humanity, the whole of life, and the entire world. Our egoic will to act independently at the expense of the whole will be overcome by an understanding that our personal interests are aligned with the whole of which we are a part. With this understanding, together we can focus our intentions and actions to create a world that works for all of us.

Our values are directly reflected in all our actions, and we no longer have the luxury of indulging in unsustainable practices. For example, when we waste resources, use toxic chemicals, purchase unsustainable products, or drive gas-guzzling cars these actions reflect values of short-term profit, instant gratification, and personal convenience—among others. All these actions are selfish in the sense that they benefit the individual at the expense of the whole. When we take such short-sighted actions we display a blatant disregard for others, the environment, and future generations. The environment is in danger, natural resources are running out, and life itself is in peril. Yet we continue to plow through our fast-paced lives taking unsustainable actions at turbo velocity.

If we wish to create sustainable systems, and a sustainable world, our future actions will have to reflect the reality of our connectedness. Our values will have to support actions that work toward our own individual short-term interests, and the long-term interest of supporting life on this planet. All members of the whole are important. The whole expresses itself through its parts, it is contained in each part, and without the parts the whole would not exist. When we value others—and all life—as we value ourselves, we take the first step toward sustainable interpersonal relationships. This in turn lays the foundations on which we can work together to create a sustainable world that values and operates for the benefit of all individuals, all life, and the whole.

Sustainable practices are essential to maintain the flow of life for the individual, the community, and the world. Together, we can discover sustainable ways to achieve our goals and create new possibilities for all. We can help each other evolve to a state of synthesis with the whole. As we shift from an isolationist paradigm to a holistic paradigm, our prior selfishness for short-term personal gain transforms to a larger long-term vision of opportunity to gain greater goods from cooperation. When we value sustainability we remember that we are one, and we focus our intentions and our actions to push the evolution of humanity toward sustainable ways of life for all.

7 CREATIVITY

Our purpose in life is to create and express ourselves in our unique and diverse ways that support the lives of others.

At our deepest level, we are creators and the architects of our world. We have the awesome ability to manifest our will in material form. Our thoughts and values drive our actions, and our actions, interpersonal relationships, and collective agreements co-create our entire world. We co-create to build societies and systems—health, housing, education, transportation, economic, etc.—that answer our collective needs. We engage in recreational activities to renew and refresh ourselves and enjoy our lives. We procreate to birth children and propagate the species, and as we grow and change we recreate and reinvent our identities. Creativity is the way we manifest life into our environment, craft our self-expression, and express our unique talents and identities. Creativity is not just reserved for art; it is our very means of survival. It is the lifeblood of existence itself, and it is the means through which we can effect transformation and change.

CREATIVITY

The life force that animates all living things is innately creative. It is driven to express itself through form, and it infuses all forms of life with its immense power. Life's purpose is to continuously evolve all forms of itself in beautiful ways. Life expresses itself through us and our creations, and it uses us to evolve itself. In this way, all living things partake of the collective body of life. Like delicate seeds, we are planted in the essential clay of creation—from which all things arise—so we may grow and co-create with life. Each person is like an individual flower that comes into this world with different characteristics and beauty that no other living thing can express. We leave our seeds in the Earth for new life to emerge. Though we eventually wither and die, we pass on our creative impulses through our will and actions while we are living and impact generations to come.

A unity perspective can be beneficial when we think about creative expression. When we adopt a larger vision for ourselves, above and beyond or small individual lives, we begin to see the vast beauty of the creative expression of all. When each of us matches our individual will with the greater will of life, we each become co-creators with life in a complex and beautiful web of diverse viewpoints and expression. Our free will allows each of us to direct our thoughts and intentions in support of life, or against it. When we manifest our will in support of life, and the survival of the whole, we co-create in alignment with life itself. When we manifest our will to destroy and inhibit creative expression of others, we fall out of alignment with the creative expression the universe and rather work to block the free flow of life like circuit breakers in an electrical system.

It is easy to believe that our actions do not affect the whole. However, our thoughts and intentions are directly reflected in the world around us, and like begets like. As previously discussed, when our thought forms are based in fear, we produce more fear in our lives. For example, an anxious person may isolate and protect herself from criticism or attack, and in the process lose opportunities to connect with people with whom she would find she has quite a bit in common. By focusing on self-protection, she notices those who would attack rather than those who would be supportive and actually attracts people who would treat her as the victim she believes herself to be. She's an easy target for a narcissist who is seeking someone to control. Taken one step further, when our societies are based in and on fear, we perpetuate that fear at a societal level. By focusing on our differences with other cultures and countries, we may lose opportunities to collaborate for collective good. We may seek to imprison and go to war with those that threaten our way of life rather than seeking mutually beneficial solutions to our shared challenges.

Fear makes us feel like victims, and thereby robs us of our truly great powers of creation. It's hard to be creative and fully express ourselves when we feel others are out to get us. We get what we give in this world both as individuals and societies—a fear-based mindset creates more fear; love creates more love. We have the power to heal the wounds of separation and isolation that have kept us feeling like victims and perpetuating fear. When our communities are based in love and collaboration rather than fear and separation, we create things that support and reflect a loving environment. We come to see that our fears were blocking our true potential, like clouds covering the brilliance of the sun. As we shift our perspective from fear to love, we can shift from victimhood to be conscious co-creators with the universe empowered by the love that connects us all.

We are all collaborators in the creation of our world—more than seven billion individuals each with infinite potential. The creator is not separate from the creation, and the parts cannot be separated from the whole. We are one body of life creating together. We have the option to co-create in support of life and all of creation, or to align ourselves with forces that oppose life. We are the ancestors of the future that is ready to be born anew. What will we create?

When we work in creative collaboration with life, we actively participate in the evolution of humanity, life, and the universe. If we wish to align ourselves with a new, holistic paradigm that integrates co-creation with life, we will have to shift our consciousness and actions. With courage, compassion, and determination, we can transform ourselves and the world as we express our individual gifts of originality. The destroyer will become the creator. The warrior will become the peaceful collaborator. We will replace our separateness with oneness and our fragmentation with wholeness. Our fear of others will transform into love of the whole. When we creatively transform our thinking and our consciousness, we are that much closer to realizing a holistic paradigm that works for the benefit of all creation.

We are not powerless, we are creators.

Now, more than ever, our entire world is in crisis, and we often feel powerless to do anything about it. Things are spinning out of control, the world is teetering on the brink of destruction, and it is difficult enough for many of us to struggle through each day. Worrying about expressing our fullest capabilities and achieving our highest creative potential seems like a luxury afforded to a select few. Apart from all that, we may feel trapped by circumstances, unable to live the life we truly want. Rather than striving to fulfill our wildest dreams, we believe we have to settle for merely getting by. Sadly, living life in this way often leaves us feeling as though we have missed the mark, and we can be left questioning everything. What if things had been different? Would my life have been better if only I had taken that path instead of this one? What could have been?

Without a doubt, life's constant challenges can be exhausting and overwhelming. However, we are only powerless if we believe that our choices and actions do not matter. We can choose not to get stuck in disempowering "what if" loops of continual questioning, or "if only" loops of second-guessing. We can stop looking outside ourselves for the source of our discontent. We can recognize that we are the sovereigns

CREATIVITY

of our destinies, and that our creativity is the means through which we can effect transformation and change—in ourselves and the world. This is not an egotistical recognition, but a claiming of the true power we hold. Instead of exchanging our power of creativity for powerlessness or helplessness, we can choose to harness it—we can choose to become active creators and co-creators of our world.

Given our increasingly crisis-filled world, it may seem absurd to suggest that we have the power to create anything that will effect positive change. We will not magically create a world without crises or challenges by simply valuing and embracing our creativity. Creativity is not meant to be understood as a panacea for all our ills, nor is it a suggestion that we should all adopt artistic lifestyles and professions. When we value creativity it is a recognition of our fundamental nature as creators—a recognition of who we really are, and a recognition of our innate power to create, transform, and change things. When we value creativity we actively participate in the creation of the world we want to live in by directing our thoughts, intentions, and actions to achieve our goals.

Creativity—our power of creation—is a great gift and a great responsibility. Our thoughts are forms of energy that shape our words and actions, and this energy travels throughout the world in a great chain reaction of life. Life's energy flows through us through our creations and it ultimately comes back to us in the great circle of life. When we choose to co-create in conjunction with the source of life and consciousness that resides within us, we embark on the creation of a world that supports the highest development of all. Whether we add our creative power to the very source of life, or not, is up to us.

8 EMPOWERMENT

By empowering others, we empower ourselves because we are all one. We can only realize our true power together.

Our freedom to create and recreate our lives empowers us to change ourselves, and thereby affect change within the world. Unfortunately, this gift of freedom can also be our greatest stumbling block. We often fear our own transformation and so we resist change—individually and collectively. When we are afraid, it is easy to fall into questioning ourselves, our decisions, and the changes that are under way. Do I really want to go through with this? Am I strong enough? What will become of me? Marianne Williamson writes in *A Return to Love*: "Our deepest fear is not that we are inadequate. Our deepest fear is that we are powerful beyond measure. It is our light, not our darkness, that most frightens us." We are not unequal to all the challenges we face, but we often fear how other people will react if we work to better ourselves and the world. We worry that others may see us as getting an inflated ego, or rising above our station in life. We worry that if we shine, we may make others may look inferior, and then, out of their own fear and resentment, they may choose to work against us. However, this is a faulty perspective. As Williamson goes on to say: "And as we let our own light shine, we unconsciously give other people permission to do the same." In other words, when we put forth our best and brightest selves, we empower others to put forth their best and brightest selves.

When we seek empowerment in this sense, we dare to overcome any fear or anxiety we may have about reaching our own highest potential. We choose to go for our dreams and then extend that expanded vision for ourselves to others. Rather than thinking that if one person wins, someone else must lose, we seek win-win outcomes. We aim to help all people express their unique talents in this world for the benefit of all society.

What would the world look like if all people were empowered? We aren't going to all become professional football players, presidents, famous actors or billionaires. The goal is not to give everyone the power of leadership, monetary power, or fame. Rather, we recognize the unique talents each person has to contribute to society. We support each other in the fulfillment of our individual roles, whatever they may be. For example, we can empower each other to be the best teacher, engineer, farmer or secretary possible or the most self-actualized parent or child or teenager. We support others as they seek to be their best and to fulfill their dreams. Of course, if a person's dream is to cause injury to others and society as a whole, we aim to help that person redirect his or her efforts towards activities that support others rather than hinder them. We aren't empowering a terrorist to be a better terrorist. Rather we are encouraging that person to recognize that we are all one body of humanity and that we can only realize our true potential in cooperation and collaboration with others.

Clearly, some people are so entrenched in their worldview of empowering themselves at the expense of whole, they are not receptive to other perspectives. Due to a long history of contrary values, society is structured to promote competition over collaboration and hierarchy over a more level playing field. Over time, however, people who experience the benefits of cooperation will seek out others who will continue to cooperate with them. Those who do not cooperate will be thereby marginalized. As more and more people begin to value the empowerment of others as well as themselves, all will benefit and fewer people will be likely to deviate from this norm.

Now is the time to reframe our approach to empowerment. Generally speaking, social movements from the left have aimed to empower people collectively at the grassroots level, and social movements from the right have focused more on the rights of the individual. While both approaches have proved useful—or not—at various times throughout history, they have undoubtedly left us with a legacy of separation and an "us versus them" mentality. Rather than looking to the traditional left or right, it is time to recognize that we are one with each other and all of creation, and that we must account for the whole.

We need to forge new ways to empower ourselves collectively, but that will also secure the rights of the individual. Both are important, but they need not be mutually exclusive, and empowerment of one group does not have to mean the disempowerment of other groups. By stepping out of our current framework of left or right, up or down, horizontal or vertical, we can see the benefit of empowerment in all directions.

By respecting all forms of life, and promoting practices that support the whole, we will arrive at new solutions to today's challenges—solutions we may never have dreamt of before. This is not to say that all changes need to be made in committees and a group context. Rather, it is a mindset in which individual and collective intentions aim to support each other and the whole. In such an environment, rather than sinking to the lowest common denominator of groupthink and uniformity, those entrepreneurs whose creativity spark new technologies and inventions may find even more support for new ideas and increased innovation as social structures evolve to support the creative expression of all.

As humanity awakens to new possibilities of empowerment and social change, old systems which were built upon an isolationist paradigm will crumble and fall. Like a caterpillar that transforms into a butterfly, we will transform into a new humanity and emerge from our chrysalis ready to participate in the creation of a new world. Realizing our connectedness to each other and all things, and valuing the power we have in unity, we will emerge as one powerful movement of social transformation. We just need to be willing to see another way, take those first steps, and the universe will usher us toward a new, empowered, holistic paradigm that supports the whole of creation.

We must use our power to cooperate, not dominate.

Thinking ourselves to be the most highly evolved creatures on the planet, we often doubt the value of the natural world, and we attempt to control nature. We promote human interests above all else, and we dominate each other, other species, and other forms of life. In our greed and quest for ever greater power, we trample those weaker than ourselves as a matter of course. When we stomp through our chaotic world with isolationist blinders on, we take actions that are counter to nature and counter to the whole. In doing this, we make our circumstances worse, and we trap ourselves in a downward spiral that will result in our demise if we do not change our ways. Using our power to control and dominate only serves to devolve, rather than evolve, humanity.

By seeking the empowerment of everyone—in all directions, at all levels—and all forms of life, we will begin to operate in new ways. We will embrace collaboration, cooperation, and co-creation with all living things. We will allow ourselves to learn from other cultures, religions, and perspectives, and to learn through the observation and preservation of other forms of life. In the words of Democritus of Abdera (c. 460-370 BC), the philosopher who actually developed the atomic theory: "In the most important concerns we are pupils of the animals. We learn spinning and mending from the spider, building from the swallow, and imitative singing from songbirds as well as from the swan and nightingale." Given the state of our world, there has never been a better time to heed the proverbs that remind us that all living things can teach us, and sometimes two heads are better than one. We will only overcome the global crises we face by facing them together, as empowered individuals and empowered collectives as one circle of life.

Our current modes of existence are in many ways dependent on interrupting and interfering with the circle of life, rather than supporting and promoting it. We wipe out forests to make furniture and paper products—paper plates, junk mail, advertisements for products we do not need—or to make parking lots and shopping malls. We destroy entire ecosystems to build vacation communities. We slaughter animals for their meat, skin, silk, and many other body parts; we breed them into distorted forms to produce more milk, meat, or silk, and for our vanity in the case of designer pets. We torture and vivisect animals in the name of experimentation and research, often in connection with chemical-filled cosmetics and beauty products that offer no real benefit to us. Many circuses still cage and abuse animals for our entertainment, and while some zoos now work to preserve endangered species, we did not start collecting animals in zoos for altruistic purposes. Without hesitation, we kill, imprison, torture, exploit, experiment on, and slaughter other forms of life for our own selfish ends. In light of this, it is hardly surprising that we are also capable of doing this to each other. The point is that our current paradigm supports the detrimental mentality that allows us to continue with these most backward ways of existence. This mentality is destroying the circle of life, and that includes us.

Ralph Waldo Emerson said of power: "All power is of one kind, a sharing in the nature of the world." Our challenge as humanity is to experience and exercise our power in this way. The time and space for destructively wielding our power over other people and other forms of life are quickly running out. We must stop interfering with the circle of life, and start supporting it. It is no longer feasible to continue interrupting the flow of energy that courses through all things, and we must stop trying to control it. Rather than using our energy in egoistic ways to dominate, divide, conquer, and control, we can remove the roadblocks we throw up and work in conjunction with the source of our power—the source of all life in the universe. Instead of crushing nature and other forms of life, we can work with them and help them to thrive. We can choose to work together, rather than subjugating each other. When we empower each other we are no longer circuit breakers in the grand matrix of universal energy, we are generators. We will no longer be like dead moons reflecting the rays of the sun, rather, we will become like the sun itself.

The new world we want to create calls not for the exercise of power over all by a few. It will be based on the power within, and that flows through, all things. We share in the energy—the power—that circulates through all things. This continuous, unending power infuses everything. It is the source by and through which individual plants and animals come into being, grow, die, return to the soil, and change into something else. This power is the foundation of the great circle of life, and ultimately, we cannot control it. It is time to exchange our power of domination for the power of cooperation and collaboration so we may join together in the empowerment of all.

The universe will empower us, if we let it.

Imagine a small child arriving at a fence. She stares at it for a while, wondering what is on the other side. She tries to peek through the cracks, but nothing comes into view. All she can see are shadows and glimmers of light. Then she looks up at the top of the fence and her heart sinks. She feels small and incapable of crossing this seemingly insurmountable barrier.

Nestling herself on the ground, she tosses around sticks and leaves that have accumulated at the bottom of the fence. She wonders why they are stuck there with her. As she arranges the twigs into the shape of a person she realizes that she is very creative, and she feels quite pleased with herself. Then it occurs to her, perhaps she can come up with a creative solution and rise above her fence predicament.

Standing up and dusting herself off, she evaluates the challenge. She finds a shorter section of fence that has a little nook in it, just perfect for a foothold. Using all the strength in her arms and legs she pushes and pulls herself up. As she nears the top, the thought pops into her head that she might not be able to get down the other side. Fear arises in her but she continues, as she is now too high to jump back down. Reaching the top, she breathes a sigh of relief. To her surprise, her father is waiting there for her, ready to lift her over to the other side.

This little child is like Dorothy in *The Wizard of Oz*. She came to realize that the power to scale the fence was in her all along. Just as Dorothy simply had to click her heels to go home, all the child had to do was get that first foothold and start climbing. However, before she could create solutions, she first had to realize that it was in her power to overcome the situation. Then, as she began climbing, she had to face her deepest fear that she was somehow inadequate to the task—just as Dorothy had to face flying monkeys and a wicked witch to overcome her fears. It was through dealing with her darkness, her fear, that the little child found her power.

So it is with all of us. When we face obstacles we are often scared we do not have the heart, brains, or courage to overcome them. The truth is that we merely need to get a bigger vision to see new possibilities, and take the first steps to lift ourselves up. Once we are willing to take those first steps, the universe—like a loving parent—will support us in our efforts. Meeting us halfway, the power of the universe will gracefully carry us to our new destination. Like the little child, we need the desire and will to solve our problems, and when we take our first steps the universe will uplift and empower us to reach our intended destination.

If we do not claim our power, others will.

Power-hungry people are like parasites waiting to suck away the power of those who are afraid to claim their birthright. When we are not willing to realize our potential, we are giving away our power. If we do not claim it someone else will. It is the awareness of this that explains the widespread production of fear in our societies. Media and propaganda are used to instill terror in us, and to keep us small. By creating an environment of fear, the power-hungry are able to gobble up and capitalize on our unclaimed power.

With courage and creativity, however, we can be pioneers of a new and beautiful world. We can choose to rise above our fears and the limited thinking that has kept us playing small. With our willingness to transform, we dissolve the witches of our own limitation and realize that nothing will save us but ourselves. With this new perspective, we are then empowered to further support those around us. With the simple intent to empower everyone, we open the floodgates to the power of the universe. We are so powerful that by swimming against the tide we can actually reverse the current.

Rather than controlling others for our own advantage, we must use our power to create synergistic collaborations among all the parts of creation. It is through loving ourselves and valuing others that we connect with the source of all power and find our innate strength. As we align our intentions with the intentions of our source, we radiate that power throughout the world. In this way, we empower the whole of creation. Withholding our power creates separation, illness, and pain. Expressing our power in co-creation with life enlightens and empowers all. Like the little child at the foot of a fence, all we need to do is take the first steps to this higher perspective. The universe will meet us there and carry us to our new lives. When we work together, each part is empowered to achieve its fullest potential, and we participate in the evolution of humanity as a whole.

CHOICE

We have the freedom to choose what we create and destroy, how we act and react, what we value, and how we live.

Everything we have created in the world is the result of our choices. In a cascading chain of events, our choices ultimately manifest in material form: we have a thought; we choose to put energy into that idea; we decide to put that idea into action; and many things come about due to that first choice and all the choices that followed. For example, when we look at a house we know someone decided to build it, and many choices were made in order for it to become a reality: the property was obtained or purchased; an architect was probably employed to draw up plans in accordance with the future homeowner's vision; builders were chosen to implement the plans and build the house; and many choices were made in respect of the building materials, finishes, and landscaping. If someone had not made that first choice to build the house, none of these other things would have happened.

CHOICE

Choices are also made on a societal scale, and the dominant worldview manifests the larger realities we are all experiencing. Our societies believe at a certain level that we must necessarily compete and fight to survive, and so we manifest an antagonistic reality rather than a cooperative one. By choosing to value an isolationist paradigm of individualism, separation, and competition over collaboration, we have created a world of nations turned against each other, depleted natural resources, a deteriorating natural world, and social, political, and economic turmoil. We have missed the mark over and over, and we are suffering for it. Absolutely everything that arises is the result of choices. By extension, we will manifest a different future by making different choices.

On a personal level, many of us have made choices that have left us feeling as though we exist in a perpetual whirlwind. We rush from one thing to the next, multitasking to meet the demands of our work, family, society, and self. Too many of us have unfulfilling jobs, and we are easily discarded by the system to meet the needs of imbalanced economies. Meanwhile, we are distracted by the constant media bombardment of advertising, television, movies, music, news, and politics.

As we struggle to get by in this chaotic environment, it is very easy to feel like a victim. We did not actively choose this—or did we? Even if we did, we could not possibly have intended these results. The good news is that, regardless of our current situation, we can choose again and change our ways and our future. There are no victims; there are only those who forget their power to choose something else. We have the ability to decide what we would like to see in the world, and the power to choose to create it. Like the Scarecrow and the Lion in *The Wizard of Oz*, we simply need the wisdom to recognize, and the courage to reclaim, the value and power of our choices.

We are all creators, and our power to make choices is like a laser that directs our intentions and energy toward the goals we set. We have the power to choose where we focus our energy and what we manifest in the material world. In each moment, we make decisions based on our beliefs and values that determine our destiny and shape our future. In other words, our ability to choose provides us with the means to shape reality. Through our individual and collective choices, we decide what will emerge into form and what will only be a fleeting thought that disappears as quickly as it arose.

We create our individual lives in the context of everyone else's choices, and together we create our collective reality. Because we have focused much of our attention on fear and separation, our world now reflects such fear and separation. The news and entertainment are filled with fear and violence, and as we consume and identify with this media our consciousness begins to reflect and reinforce these destructive forces. That which receives our attention is magnified and strengthened in the world if we do not question it. However, this dire situation we find ourselves in is truly a gift. We do not have to succumb to the paralysis of fear, nor do we have to feel helpless and doomed. Rather, we have the good fortune to be able to use our current chaos as a catalyst for change. In our suffering from misguided choices, we can take new aim and try again—we have the ability to make new choices. If we were comfortable, why would we choose differently? Our discomfort encourages us to change our ways. As we are faced with many ongoing global dilemmas, we have the opportunity to align our future choices and actions with a higher vision for humanity. By choosing love over fear, and making choices that support the sustainability of the whole, we will magnify love, sustainability, and unity in the world.

Now is the time to choose again, and to make better choices that will support and benefit the whole of creation. Our choices can no longer be made only in support of ourselves, our families, our communities, our countries, and our species. We have the power to make choices from an elevated perspective, creating our lives in the context of the whole interconnected world. It is up to us whether we decide to make choices that support a healthy and sustainable world, or to make choices that continue down our current path. It is as simple as choosing to switch on a light to illuminate a room, or choosing to switch the light off and leave the room in darkness. By choosing to give our attention and energy to that which reflects a holistic paradigm, we choose to enlighten humanity and evolve.

We may become gripped by fear, but we can choose to overcome it.

In our media-saturated world, the creation and perpetuation of fear is prevalent and many companies and others in power benefit by controlling the masses through fear tactics and agendas. Dramatic and often terrifying images and ideas are broadcast and published in a 24-hour news cycle. In reaction to their fear, people advocate war and the vast business that it has become for suppliers and governments. We fear diseases and buy pharmaceuticals at the first onset of a mysterious symptom that we read about on the Internet or saw in a commercial. When people get depressed about what they see in the news, they often opt for the antidepressant shown in a commercial that same evening. While there are great benefits to many pharmaceuticals, casual use to counter discontent with the state of the world and our lives only serves to keep us from implementing change. Fear keeps the masses in check and discourages them from taking actions contrary to the will of those in power.

For many, a fear-based mindset has become the new normal. We fear terrorism, economic instability, climate change, diseases, unemployment, the weather, and each other. Desperate for information on the latest threat or disaster, we remain glued to our televisions, radios, and online media—watching, listening, waiting, and anticipating the worst. In our fearful state, we have created a growing demand for fear-based programming that the mass media is more than willing to exploit. Our access to news, events, and stories from across the globe is in fact empowering, but if we cling to fear—and continue to demand fear-based programming—we are only serving to reinforce fear-based thinking.

The global fear that is permeating our societies can feel paralyzing. It takes great courage to choose a different path, but all we really need to do is take the first step. By choosing to overcome fear, we begin to change. When we choose not to act in fear, we more readily arrive at creative solutions that will transform our circumstances for the better—rather than worsening and devolving them. All that is required is for each of us to individually make that personal choice and put it into action.

Fear itself is a choice. When we choose to act in fear we are reactive, and more likely to take impulsive and shortsighted actions. In contrast, when we reflect on our circumstances with objectivity and equanimity, we can rise above our fears and see new possibilities from a new perspective. It is entirely within our power to recognize the global challenges we face, take responsibility for our past choices, and respond with appropriate actions—without being swept up in waves of fear and anxiety.

When we choose to overcome our individual fears, we are supporting a larger worldview that values love over fear. By choosing to work together to create a new world that matches our values—love over fear, connectedness over separation, choice and responsibility over apathy—we are reclaiming our authority. When we set our new vision into action we become the authors of our destiny. In this way, we inspire and empower others to take a stand with us, and, together, with shared intentions, we can choose to create a new world.

We cannot abdicate our responsibility and expect positive results.

One of the most destructive choices we can make is to abdicate our decision-making authority. As we go through life distracted by the mass media, or bewildered by our circumstances, it is easy to let others make choices for us, or to leave things up to chance. In times of crisis—such as these we are living through—we can feel so frightened and overwhelmed by everything that it often seems that the easiest thing to do is nothing. However, by choosing to let others take control of our decision-making we are choosing to give away our power, and by default we are choosing to live the life that someone else has chosen for us. Those who are not actively engaged in life abandon their power as creators, and choose to live in the wake of decisions made by others.

Choosing to align our actions with our values can be one of the hardest choices we ever have to make. It takes great courage, but we are not alone. We are all in this together and, together, we can muster the courage for all of us. As one brave soul starts to create a world that works for all, a brick is laid in the path, and others are emboldened to follow that lead. When we have the courage to become trailblazers, we encourage others to do the same.

We must not be afraid to make hard choices or to advocate change. Many of us may ask: Who am I to make an important decision at a time like this? The better question is: Who am I not to? The future of the world is depending on each and every one of us to choose rightly. We are all caretakers of the world, and for too long we have not taken our great responsibility seriously. We are collectively responsible for creating our circumstances, and the only way we can change things is to become co-creators of a better future. It is up to each of us to ensure that we do our part.

The key is to be an active participant in whatever ways we can. Not everyone will have the precise skills or expertise to take on the technical challenges we face, but each of us has the power to decide to cooperate with others to accomplish what needs to be done. We do not all have the aptitude or training to be rocket scientists or brain surgeons or political leaders, but we can all choose to cooperate with others to overcome our global crises, set humanity on a better path, and get the job done in the most life-sustaining ways possible. Certain individuals will be better suited to carrying out certain tasks, but we can all choose to support the highest good for all. We can choose to empower others and ourselves by joining forces to find creative solutions to the challenges we face today.

Our societies are imprisoned by our mistakes, faulty logic, bad choices, and our destructive and divisive isolationist paradigm. However, we have the power to set our collective intentions in the right direction, and to put our energy and actions into solutions based on love rather than fear. When we have the courage to make better choices on a personal level, that energy ripples out into the universe and gives others the courage and strength to join us. By taking charge of ourselves, we take charge of the whole.

The whole of humanity and creation can be steered in a new direction when one imaginative soul dares to choose another way. Because all things are interconnected in one body of life, the choice of one person can have an instantaneous effect on everything. Making that choice makes a difference—whether or not it sets in motion a series of events that overtly leads to substantive change. What we choose to eat for breakfast, what we choose to say to a sales clerk, how we react to the news—all these choices matter because our choices, big or small, collectively create our reality and they affect the realities of everyone else. By choosing to act in love, compassion, and kindness in all we do, we are setting the foundation for a better, cooperative future for all.

The game of life

Choosing, acting, responding to the consequences, and choosing again—this is how we play the game of life. As humans, we are all members of the same team playing a shared game. The optimal outcome of the game of life will not be achieved by individuals making choices and decisions that are solely in their own self-interest at the expense of the whole. We know that optimal results will be achieved for our team when all the players cooperate and work together. This can be seen in the context of team sports. If the stars of any team decide to try to win a game on their own—and choose not to work with their teammates—the result will often be a loss for the team. So it is for the team of humanity playing the game of life.

The world used to be a place that could withstand us playing the game using strategies of extreme individualism and egoistic self-centeredness. In fact, these strategies were quite profitable and materially rewarding for many individuals and a few nations. The problem is that the world has changed, but we have not. We no longer have an abundance of natural resources, seemingly unlimited space and time, and a pristine environment to exploit. Continuing to play only for our own self-interest with disregard for the larger context in which we live may indeed still provide huge, short-term profits for a few, but the cost to the many is becoming too high to bear. These myopic and self-centered strategies are not viable in the long-term.

The playing field has changed, and if we hope to survive we have to devise a new game plan. We learn and grow through making choices, facing the results of our choices, and taking responsibility for them. By now, we should understand we can no longer play for fun, games, and short-term benefit, as if we are carefree children in a playground. The stakes are much too high. By continuing to play by the old rules, we are only moving ourselves closer and closer to the brink. We are in our final hour, and shortsighted, immature choices are no longer a luxury we can afford. Our future choices will determine the future of our species. If we do not choose rightly, we will continue to threaten our own lives, our societies, and civilization as we know it. Life itself is now on the line. The stakes cannot get any higher, and we need to start playing smarter and wiser.

When we choose to play a new, mature game, learning from our mistakes, we will create the possibility of establishing new modes of existence that sustain all life on this planet. Rather than continuing to play a zero-sum game that will likely not go on for much longer, we can choose to play a sustainable, inclusive, and cooperative game of life into the future. With the wisdom of learning from our past missteps, we will begin to set new rules whereby we call can interact for mutual benefit in the long run.

To make better choices, we must listen to our bodies and our instincts.

Many of us are so used to thinking and choosing only with our minds, we have lost the wisdom that our bodies can afford us. We try to think things through, weighing all of the pros and cons, completely ignoring our intuition and instincts. As part of a society that values reason and intellect, we have become accustomed to suppressing and ignoring what our bodies tell us, and often cut ourselves off from some of the natural intelligence our bodies possess. On top of that, we have learned to distrust ourselves and our ability to make good decisions, because we have made so many bad choices in the past. We may believe we need to really think things through in order to avoid the mistakes of our past. What we forget is that many of those poor choices were not made holistically, and as such, many of them were bound to be bad.

By moving out of our head and into our body in the moment of choice, we can overcome any anxiety we have around making choices. Rather than living full of fear about the future, we can step into the present moment and think with our whole being. This is not to say that we should not use reason and intellect to solve our problems. Of course, we can use the mind to evaluate the circumstances and information at hand. In addition, however, we should also look to our heart to connect to the greater good, and our gut to direct us to the right course of action that is in alignment with our values. For example, have you ever thought that from a logical perspective and according to society, you should do one thing, but your intuition and gut feeling is to do another? Perhaps your heart is more aligned with your morals than, for example, the intellectual short-term pursuit of profit or personal gain. In a more concrete example, advertisements and social norms may make a particular food popular, but you find that it makes you feel poorly. These are only a few examples, but when we take an expanded view and a holistic approach, listening to our intuition and our bodies, we can begin to follow our natural instincts and the natural universal order, rather than merely being guided by existing social constructs and norms.

As the common phrase goes, (often attributed to Albert Einstein although not confirmed), we cannot solve our problems with the same level of thinking that created them. By using our whole being to make choices, we assist life in transforming our world. When we choose to let life flow through us—rather than trying to control it—the results will naturally support the greater good. We will relax into the natural order of things and let the intelligence of the universe work through us. We will rise above destructive social norms and practices and permit the greatest forces of the universe to undo the mistakes of our faulty choices, and we will thereby revolutionize the world.

We can use our choices to become agents of change.

We have the opportunity to be agents of change in the evolution of humanity. We can remain prisoners of our faulty thinking and choices, or we can make the courageous decision to participate in the unfolding of a new world. The choice is ours. In choosing to adopt a new paradigm that supports a healthy and sustainable world, we are choosing to be a transformer like Shiva, the ancient Hindu deity, who represents aspects of both creation and destruction. We become a catalyst for the falling away of the old and the emergence of what is to come. As we act in ways that support life, each other, the environment, and the world, we begin to undo the past harm we have collectively caused in exchange for a brighter future.

Ultimately, we must decide as individuals whether or not we will support the greater whole of which we are a part. The time we take to make that choice is up to us. We can suffer by delaying that choice, or we can choose rightly—now. Once we make that decision and relax into our transformation, our individual choices begin to align with those that support our collective evolution. My will becomes thy will—and we begin to act as one.

10. INTEGRITY

*Everything is integrated—inherently complete,
undivided parts of the whole. When we remember our oneness,
we act with integrity to the benefit of all.*

The word integrity is frequently used to refer to honesty and adherence to ethical standards. When we act with integrity, we honor our word and act with moral character. On a personal level, if we do things that go against our morals—outward actions that do not match our internal value system—we create internal divisions and conflicts. When we are at odds internally, we fall out of integrity with ourselves. On a societal level, we also make commitments to behave in accordance with agreements with other people, communities, businesses, and nations. If we break those promises, we are out of integrity with others. Integrity can also be viewed as a state of being whole and refer to the integrated and connected nature of our world. When we remember our oneness—that we are a small part in a large universe of creation— we act in alignment with the whole of which we are a part.

Our current isolationist paradigm can undermine both our moral character and the integrity of the whole. Our societies—and we as individuals—continue to act in ways that may have short-term benefit but are self-destructive in the long run. For example, in the quest for increasingly scarce natural resources, rather than cooperating to solve the problems caused by this scarcity, countries go to war and allow others to lay waste to the environment. As we exhaust the world's resources and make choices that damage our environment, we threaten the future of other species and humanity. On an individual level, we may find that our jobs require us to do things that we would not do if the choice were left up to us, but rather than speaking out and maintaining our integrity, we choose to go along with the program for a quiet life, or to protect our standard of living. Many of us choose to focus on our own immediate needs and desires, and in doing this we often ignore the good of the whole, forgetting that we ourselves benefit from the well-being of others and our environment. If we do not start respecting the integrity and integrated nature of all life, and adopt such values as a basis for our conduct, there may come a time when life will no longer be able to sustain us.

We live by social agreements and contracts.

Humans are social beings. We depend on each other for survival, and every society operates within a complex network of intra-societal agreements made among the members at all levels—individual, family, group, community, and country. Members of communities have unwritten agreements which can determine local social norms, mores, and practices. These understandings determine acceptable behavior within the community, for example, how we queue for a bus or train, whether or not we clap our hands at the end of a performance, the etiquette of local hospitality, and even what is or is not to be eaten. Of course, formal agreements and contracts can also be made among individuals and businesses to outline the proper functioning of some defined interaction or transaction, and they can be made to cover almost any situation imaginable. We even make agreements with ourselves, usually in an effort to change or improve our lives, for example, to eat healthier food, to exercise, or to save money. By making these agreements we enter into formal and informal contracts which define a set of rules for our conduct, and we generally accept that honoring our agreements and contracts equates to acting with integrity.

At the broadest level, when nations are formed and governed by an overall set of rules that acknowledges the power of the rulers and the ruled it is understood that the nation has a social contract. The state and the people contract with each other, and they are both responsible for upholding the social contract. In other words, people agree to accept political authority and to operate under a set of rules in exchange for the social contract which grants them certain freedoms, rights, and protections in relation to each other, the state, and other states or countries. Societies governed by a social contract are unlike dictatorships or totalitarian states in which everyone has agreed—often by force or default—that all the power will be held by the dictator or central authority. When a social contract is violated by an individual, that person may be penalized or lose his freedom, and a state that violates the social contract may be held to account by the people.

Regardless of whether a country operates by social contract or not, intra-societal rules are often codified in laws that govern the functioning of society. These can cover a wide variety of topics including the rules of the road, political processes, financial systems, and all other areas that society has agreed should be governed by law. On an international scale, our inter-societal agreements outline how countries relate to each other in terms of their economies, trade, laws, and security. For example, many countries have agreed that certain interest rates in their national economies are affected by the London Interbank Offered Rate (LIBOR), and many currency exchange rates are tied to other currencies. Trade agreements may provide certain rules for conducting business and exchanging goods and services. Extradition treaties allow for the repatriation of citizens who flee justice in their own country. Security treaties can, for example, allow countries to share information about their citizens, form military alliances in the event of war, and regulate the sale, exchange, and provision of weapons.

In essence, through agreements both simple and complex, we have created rules for how we interact within and between groups of all sizes. These agreements are the basis for our social structures, and generally speaking—i.e., when all parties have agreed and accepted the contract—we act with integrity by upholding our end of the agreement. When we fail to maintain our side of the bargain the agreement or contract is broken, and we fall out of integrity.

Social contracts can be changed and gained.

One of the challenges faced by many societies today is that some of our collective agreements reflect an outdated isolationist paradigm. Such outdated agreements manifest imbalances across societies and environments, resulting in the spread of inequality and environmental degradation. Not only have these imbalances led to the breakdown of the social fabric in many places, they may lead to our ultimate demise if we do not shift our thinking and our paradigm. If we hope to have a future, we cannot continue in these ways.

A most glaring example of imbalance is the rampant greed and consumerism plaguing many societies at the expense of the environment. In the pursuit of material gain, it is easy to forget the environment, our countries, our societies, our communities, and even our families. Money-driven decisions and practices are not only valued by consumers who want to acquire as much as they can, but also by producers who knowingly sacrifice the environment and the physical, mental, and financial health of their workforces in the race to produce more and more in order to gain bigger and bigger profits.

We know such practices are unhealthy for individuals and the entire world, and we know something must change to be sustainable in the long run.

Our social contracts often reflect the values of those in power, but the good news is that social contracts are subject to change. The establishment may choose to grant new rights or freedoms of its own accord, or the people may choose to demand them. If the cost of abiding by rules and values we do not agree with is outweighed by the benefits we stand to gain, then we can choose to deviate from the social norm and work to change it. In societies that do not have an agreed social contract, people can join forces to lobby the government for one. When enough people disagree with the status quo and they choose to promote and act in accordance with their personal values, new laws can be enacted to reflect the new values and the will of the people.

Over the last two hundred years we have seen examples of beneficial changes to social contracts in many countries. These changes include the abolition of slavery, universal suffrage, and civil rights movements. Other major changes to social contracts in the 20th century were achieved in Europe and North America by trade union movements that fought for workers' rights, child labor laws, and health and safety regulations. In Asia and Africa, anti-colonial struggles led to the emancipation of former colonies, thereby altering the social contract and allowing the colonies to establish themselves as free nations. More recently, people are coming together to demand environmental justice, social equality, and animal rights.

Granted, as change emerges, there can be great resistance from those who favor old ways. Movements emerge to enforce old fundamentalist perspectives, to deny equality and to fight new laws that would enforce more collaborative and holistic viewpoints. Corporations lobby government to reduce regulation and the wealthiest individuals fund political campaigns to influence legislation. However, when a critical mass of people come together in support of new values, we can turn the tide of social norms. This can lead to anything from the creation and fulfillment of emerging markets—for example, "green" and sustainable services and organic, biodegradable, and recyclable products—to changes in the law and new social contracts being agreed. By acting together, we can be the catalysts for evolving social contracts and evolving humanity. When we act with integrity to support and protect the integrity of the whole, we are integral players in the manifestation of a new holistic paradigm that will work for all of us.

A holistic approach integrates apparent opposites.

In Chinese philosophy, the concept of Yin and Yang describes the universe, our world, and ourselves as dynamic systems of forces continually balancing themselves. It suggests that apparently competing and contrary forces can be understood as complementary and interdependent. Not only are they inherently interconnected, such opposing forces give rise to each other. For example, the shadow is merely an absence of light. As the Earth rotates around our Sun, the elements of light and dark manifest on our planet, yet they come from a single, dynamic system. Fire and water, male and female, hot and cold—all can be viewed as reflections of one source shifting and taking different forms under varying conditions and circumstances.

The Yin Yang symbol also has a dot representing the opposite force within each element; there is a small black dot in the white half and a small white dot in the black half. This symbolizes a balance between the two opposites with a little bit of the other intermingled in each side. Together, they make a unified whole.

In the thick of direct conflict between polarized viewpoints, it can be challenging to see commonality and interdependence among the parties. If we are stuck in an "us versus them" mentality, common ground is difficult to find. It as if we are only seeing the Yin side or the Yang side, but not both sides swirling together and somewhat overlapping. However, by rising above the conflict to understand the interests of both sides, it is possible to arrive at compromises and new approaches that bring balance and new possibilities to all. Our paradigm and worldview, including our values, either enable such an integrative, holistic perspective or prohibit it. When we adopt values rooted in the oneness and interconnectedness of all things, a more holistic, elevated approach becomes possible. Otherwise, we may get stuck in a limited view of just the black or just the white rather than the two working together in a push and pull of interconnected, interdependent forces.

Our own actions can also manifest as either positive or negative, depending on our values and worldview. For example, globalization can be beneficial under a holistic paradigm, providing people with the opportunity to collaborate and help each other in ways previously unimaginable. On the other hand, if domination and control of others takes priority over collaboration, globalization can result in negative consequences. Of course, what is viewed as positive and negative also changes depending on our values. A corporation seeking to increase its profits may view corporate domination in other counties as positive, while the people who face resulting pollution and environmental degradation will view it as negative. Our values shape our approach to life and, depending on our worldview, can produce very different results.

Polarities can be found in everything, including Global Values themselves. For instance, on one level the value of freedom may seem to be in diametric opposition to the value of community. If one wishes to be free, wouldn't the freedom to make one's own choices be prioritized over choices that support the community? From an integrative, holistic perspective, however, such dichotomies can be viewed as complementary and symbiotic. We acknowledge the inherent tension between the desire for individual freedoms, on the one hand, and the need for community and, for example, collective national security, on the other. Without coming together to implement security systems and protocols, we may not be able to fully enjoy our individual freedoms within society. Therefore, we agree to certain security measures, which may restrict our personal freedoms such as rules and procedures for air travel. We make such trade-offs in order to protect our freedom to express our viewpoints, practice freedom of religion, and enjoy freedom of the press. Likewise, while democratic principles uphold our individual rights and freedom, they also promote equal rights, and opportunity for all. We can value freedom in the context of community structures that support both the individual and the whole.

Ultimately, our goal is to find a marriage and balance of the polarities in ourselves and the world: masculine and feminine, light and dark, and even heaven and hell. Global Values, and the value of integrity in particular, can serve as a vehicle for such understanding and a framework for applying a holistic perspective to our lives. By adopting this worldview, we come to recognize that apparent opposites are part of one greater whole—two sides of the same coin.

We all have the opportunity to act with integrity.

Each of us has the opportunity for both integrity within ourselves and integrity with others, in alignment with the integrity—or integrated nature—of all that is. Inwardly, we choose whether or not to align with our own values and commitments to ourselves. Outwardly, we choose whether or not to uphold the rules and laws of our societies, and whether or not to honor our agreements and contracts with others. Finally, we align our personal and societal integrity with the integrated nature of the whole. To do this, we adopt values that support a healthy and sustainable world, and choose to serve as an integral part of the whole. As we each individually act in accordance with values that support a healthy and sustainable world, we find others who share those values. As we join forces to manifest our shared values, a world begins to emerge that reflects our inner beliefs and desires. In this way, we integrate our inner world with the outer.

Valuing integrity, and honoring the integrity and oneness of the whole, is neither a negation of our individuality and diversity, nor is it a drive toward homogenization. The goal is not to end our individuality, but to respect and support the uniqueness and individuality of all things. Just as each cell in the human body takes on certain roles for the proper functioning of the whole, each person fulfills certain functions within society and life itself. We are integral parts of the body of life, and when our diverse roles serve the benefit of the collective, they serve us. To value integrity is to experience our separate material forms while resting in the knowledge of our connection to all things. When we take an integrative, holistic approach to the polarities and conflicts we face in our world, we emerge from the night of illusion to the birth of a new world. When we take actions based in these principles, our smaller self-centered selves are incinerated by our commitment to the whole, and together we rise like a phoenix from our own ashes. With such transformation, we create the possibility of living in community and communion with each other, integrated and whole, embraced by the power of an all-encompassing love.

11
A CALL TO ACTION

Change begins with us.

Many of us are frustrated with the world in which we live. We may feel as if we must fix things out there if we want to be happy; not to mention survive as a species. This approach of looking outside ourselves for a solution, however, is never fully successful because it addresses only the effects rather than the root cause of the problem. Every thought we have manifests as a piece of the world that surrounds us – whether it be in the way people treat us individually or the social structures that are implemented for society as a whole. Together, we create our reality with our thoughts and perspectives about the world. When we operate under a paradigm of disconnection from others, we produce more divisions and discord. When we adopt values that recognize the oneness and interconnection of all things, we create the possibility of a healthy and sustainable world.

If we want to change the world, we must first take responsibility for our own thoughts and actions. By shifting from a worldview of individualism and separation to a paradigm grounded in a holistic approach, we take the first step in our transformation. When we think we live in a world of "us versus them" and "me versus other", it necessarily follows that we attack and protect ourselves against the other. With these attack thoughts, we manifest vengeance in the world. When we see ourselves as one with all things, and experience the life force and love that unites us all, we manifest love in the world. The healing of our divisions and discord lies within us. We must merely change our minds.

A quiet mind enables transformation.

In today's hectic world, our thoughts can tend to race to keep up. Our minds are often filled with thoughts stemming from our fears and anxieties in daily life. In an effort to control our circumstances, we may think the same unproductive thoughts over and over again. Why did he say that to me? Was I wrong in doing this or that? How can I get my way? While self-reflection can be productive, our minds can somewhat obsessively repeat thoughts that do not produce positive results in our lives.

Practices of mindfulness, meditation, prayer, and yoga have been around for centuries and are gaining popularity around the world to help people deal with stress and bring peace and equanimity to daily life. To some people, such practices may seem to be complicated, difficult or even overwhelming. Some may think they need special training or a spiritual or religious teacher to even begin. While classes and guidance can be useful, it is also very effective to simply sit and be still. By doing so, we become conscious about our racing minds and gain the ability to slow down, become centered, and connect with our fundamental nature. We reach beyond our exterior, superficial self to experience our deeper connection to life and the love that connects us all.

For a simple meditation practice, it may be helpful to focus on one of the values identified in this book.

1. Set a timer for twenty minutes, preferably when you wake up in the morning. If twenty minutes seems too long, try starting with just five minutes. Five minutes alone will be enough to guide your thought forms throughout the day.

2. Read one of the values, perhaps starting with: "Unity - Together we make up one body of life."

3. Sit comfortably in a chair with your spine upright and your feet flat on the floor, your hands gently resting on your legs and palms facing upward and open. Close your eyes. Relax your jaw, face and shoulders.

4. Repeat the phrase out loud a few times. For example, "Unity - Together we make up one body of life."

5. Close your mouth and breathe through your nose, if possible. This type of breathing helps to slow down the nervous system. Rest your attention on the

breath drawing in and out of your nose. That focused attention will help you to stay present.

6. Feel life moving through you. Feel the energy in your hands. Once you can feel the energy in your hands, expand your awareness to the energy in your whole body.

7. Repeat the phrase mentally a few times—just silently to yourself. "Unity - Together we make up one body of life." Don't worry about doing this right or trying hard to concentrate. Your thoughts will naturally drift away to what you might eat for lunch or an errand that you need to do. When you realize that you have drifted away, repeat the word "Unity" and return to focusing on your breath drawing in and out of your nose.

8. Try to watch your thoughts as if you were secretly watching someone else's thoughts in a video. Be curious as to where your mind drifts and gently bring it back to watching your breath and the value of Unity.

9. Continue with this practice for five to twenty minutes and end your practice with a feeling of gratitude for the time to connect with your deeper sense of self and your connection to the whole. Throughout the day, you may wish to remind yourself of the value of Unity and its meaning in your life.

Repeat this practice daily, focusing on one value each day as follows:

A CALL TO ACTION

UNITY—Together we make up one body of life. Our diversity is a celebration of all that is. Together, we are whole.

COMMUNITY—Because we are one, individuals acting in isolation are often ineffective. By joining forces with others, we will realize our full potential.

LIFE—Life energizes and moves all things. The continuity of life is the core of our existence.

FREEDOM—Freedom is a natural right. Democratic principles are the foundation of social justice.

CONNECTION—All things have a profound impact on each other: global economies, cultures, environments, political systems, and our minds, bodies, and spirits.

SUSTAINABILITY—Sustainable practices are essential to maintain the flow of life for the individual, the community, and the world.

CREATIVITY—Our purpose in life is to create and express ourselves in our unique and diverse ways that support the lives of others.

EMPOWERMENT—By empowering others, we empower ourselves because we are all one. We can only realize our true power together.

CHOICE—We have the freedom to choose what we create and destroy, how we act and react, what we value, and how we live.

INTEGRITY—Everything is integrated - inherently complete, undivided parts of the whole. When we remember our oneness, we act with integrity to the benefit of all.

A meditation practice, such as the one just described, will help you to calm your mind and focus on what you wish to manifest in the world. We may feel like we are very separate minds with very different agendas. But when we quiet our minds, we come to realize that we are merely expressions of one mind, one life, and one integrated whole. In such moments of inner peace and stillness, we dissolve our barriers to happiness and experience the love that connects us all.

As we heal ourselves, we heal the world.

Most of us came into this world quite happy. As babies and children, we naturally had much joy. As we grew up, however, we had painful experiences and grew to doubt ourselves and perhaps feel we may not deserve love and happiness. We tried to protect ourselves from others hurting us and built up blocks both within ourselves and around us for protection. These walls and divisions may have been helpful at times, but over time they may keep us from being fully alive and experiencing all the joys life has to offer.

The good news is that since we are the ones who created such mental obstacles, we have the power to remove them. Meditation, introspection, contemplation and a still mind help us to begin to see the blocks that we have created. By shifting one's viewpoint from one of separation and isolation to a paradigm based on the unity and interconnection of all that is, the blocks that keep us separate are revealed.

A CALL TO ACTION

We come to realize that we must let go of our narrow identification with our individual selves in order to join the love and power of the universe that is always available. As we join in this new paradigm of unity and community, our ego begins to dissolve but it fights every step of the way. It is as if our ego is the Wicked Witch of the West in the story of *The Wizard of Oz*. She throws obstacles in our way to keep us from returning home to our true selves. Dorothy, the innocent child within each of us, however, has the power and resourcefulness to easily dissolve the Wicked Witch with a bucket of water. Our innocence dissolves the ego with the essence of life that flows through us, renews us and refreshes us. We come to recognize that the Wicked Witch is not outside ourselves, but a shadow of our true self—the dark side of our true nature that keeps us from realizing our full potential.

Global Values are based upon the concept that everything in the entire universe has a single source and that our inner most selves are not only connected to that source but are that source itself. When our awareness is unblocked and free, we realize that source is not out there somewhere, but rather deep within ourselves. Like a young, innocent child in a story book, we come to understand that we have had the power to transform our circumstances all along.

We begin to recognize the continuity of life—flowing through us and all things—as the core of our existence. Ever since the big bang that initiated the universe, life moved out from its singularity and took form in matter. That initial vibration still resonates and travels through all things as life flows from one thing to the next. Our self-awareness allows us to choose whether to align with that which supports life and its evolution or that which inhibits it. Through introspection, meditation, and contemplation, we aim to be liberated from the smaller self to align with a larger vision that recognizes our connection to all.

A revolution of values will transform the world.

Global Values are intended to serve as a framework through which we can transform our thinking, and thereby transform our world. By adopting these values and aligning our actions with such moral convictions, we create the possibility of manifesting a healthy and sustainable environment. A monumental transformation of society is emerging, grounded in our shift from values based on separation and isolation to a new paradigm based on the oneness and interconnectedness of all things. Dr. Martin Luther King, Jr. called for such a revolution of values many decades ago. On April 4, 1967, exactly one year before his assassination, Dr. King delivered his first major anti-war speech entitled "Beyond Vietnam" in which he called for a revolution of values supporting a love for all mankind:

> A genuine revolution of values means in the final analysis that our loyalties must become ecumenical rather than

> sectional. Every nation must now develop an overriding loyalty to mankind as a whole in order to preserve the best in their individual societies.
>
> This call for a worldwide fellowship that lifts neighborly concern beyond one's tribe, race, class, and nation is in reality a call for an all-embracing and unconditional love for all mankind.

These words are as applicable to today's challenges as they were then. King's call for a revolution in values is still being answered since it is a challenging path to take. While such a change of mind is simple, it can challenge everything that we believe about the world. In the face of conflict and injustice, people who are not willing to make a radical shift in perspective tend to either adopt an attitude of complacency and apathy or they resort to violence to stamp out the opposition. In fact, complacency on the part of many opens the door to those who wish to resort to violence. The apathy of the many enables the violence of the few.

Today, many people around the world face intolerance toward different beliefs and practices. Difficulties and violence arise due to divided sides that are so polarized they are no longer open to discussions with one another. The key to bridging these seemingly impossible divides is to face such polarization with a revolution of love for one another. We must forgive ourselves and each other for past transgressions if we wish to end our long dream of disaster. Only by rising above our polarized views and treating each other with respect and dignity can we hope to have meaningful discussion, find common ground and fulfill peaceful revolution.

King further calls for a "shift from a 'thing-oriented' society to a 'person-oriented' society" and his words have even greater meaning now.

> Increasingly, by choice or by accident, this is the role our nation has taken, the role of those who make peaceful revolution impossible by refusing to give up the privileges and the pleasures that come from the immense profits of overseas investments. I am convinced that if we are to get on to the right side of the world revolution, we as a nation must undergo a radical revolution of values. We must rapidly begin the shift from a thing-oriented society to a person-oriented society. When machines and computers, profit motives and property rights, are considered more important than people, the giant triplets of racism, extreme materialism, and militarism are incapable of being conquered.

While such a shift has yet to fully manifest, the dire status of the world demands that we change our ways. As such a revolution of values emerges, it causes us to question the fairness and justice of many of our past and present policies and beliefs. We must reassess our individual and collective practices to better suit the evolution of humanity as a whole, shifting from money-driven values to people-driven values.

We must move away from short term individual gain at expense of the whole to long term sustainable practices for all. Although society is in general operating under an outdated paradigm of separation and isolationism, a minority who dare to challenge the status quo and make their voices be heard can have a revolutionary effect. Many people have already awoken to the realization of their connection to all and are actively living these values. As more people join this values-based movement, the scales will tip toward positive social transformation.

With our hearts, minds, and courage, we lead the way.

Now is the time for a paradigm shift driven by a revolution of values. The longer we wait, the longer we will suffer because we are denying the truth of who we really are. We are inextricably bound together as one body of life. The love of the universe—the one song of creation—connects us all. We can choose to be an instrument of life or a hindrance. We can choose love or we can choose to remain in fear, blocking our awareness to the love that surrounds us. If we choose the later, we will experience pain as life works around us. If we choose to join in this movement, we will experience the love that the universe has to offer. The choice is ours.

Like Dorothy in the *Wizard of Oz*, we dreamed we could find happiness somewhere over the rainbow and got swept away by a cyclone of change. We embarked on a creative adventure, but we lost our way. Each character in our journey—like the Lion, the Scarecrow, the Tin Man, the Good Witch of the East, the Wicked Witch of the West, the Wizard, and Dorothy herself—represents an aspect of our selves that seems unfulfilled. Like the Tin Man who sought a heart, the Scarecrow who sought a brain, and the Cowardly Lion who sought courage, we sought answers outside ourselves, only to find that we have possessed the answers all along; we had only fallen asleep to the truth of who we really are. As we each reclaim and integrate those aspects of ourselves that had been forgotten or shut down—our hearts, minds, and courage—we finally wake up to experience the love of the universe that travels through and connects all things. When we awaken from our slumber, which for some has been a nightmare, we can rest in the knowledge that we are empowered to correct our ways. The path to our transformation lies within our own hearts and minds.

Throughout our life's journey, we have the opportunity to contribute to the process of reintegration of the whole. It is our responsibility to re-member—to mentally piece back together—our oneness and unified nature. By loving one another as ourselves, we will evolve to a new state of being through peaceful discourse and curtail the violence and hatred that is currently manifesting throughout the world. It takes great vision to imagine—and courage to trust—that a new and beautiful world filled with love can emerge from our current predicament. With an open heart, an open mind, and the courage to lead the way, may we remember who we really are, united as one. Together we will realize our full potential. Together we return to the peace and love at the heart of our existence, like the comfort of coming home.

ABOUT THE AUTHOR

Karin Miller was born in Jackson, Michigan, USA, in 1967. For over ten years in early adulthood, Karin suffered from debilitating anxiety and depression. In her search for a sense of overall wellbeing, she sought help and healing from many different teachings and traditions—spirituality, philosophy, psychology, meditation and yoga. Ultimately, she saw a common thread among all traditions; people should love and treat each other as they would themselves because all people and living things are connected as one body of life. She learned that fear, such as her anxiety, blocks one's awareness of the love that connects us all. Having transformed her own life, Karin went on to graduate from the University of Michigan Law School and currently resides in Southern California where she serves as Vice President and General Counsel of a digital media consortium.

Made in the USA
Lexington, KY
18 August 2016